Declared to be ~~My~~

R. C. Sproul

PRAYING FOR THE WORLD

UNDERSTANDING GOD'S HEART
FOR THE NATIONS

Jesus was sent to
fulfil _all_ righteousness.

10 Publishing
a division of 10 of those.com

Previously published in 1999 and 2012 by OMF International
10 West Dry Creek Circle, Littleton CO 80120,
under the title: *World Prayer, 30 Days of Devotionals.*

Copyright © 2017 by 10Publishing

First published in Great Britain in 2017

British Library Cataloguing in Publication Data

A record for this book is available from the British Library

ISBN: 978-1-911272-59-5
Designed by Diane Warnes
Printed in Denmark by Nørhaven, Viborg

10Publishing, a division of 10ofthose.com
Unit C, Tomlinson Road, Leyland, PR25 2DY, England
Email: info@10ofthose.com
Website: www.10ofthose.com

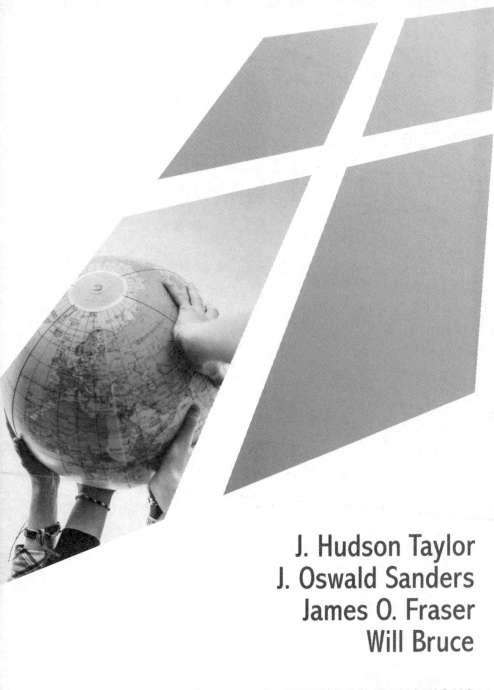

J. Hudson Taylor
J. Oswald Sanders
James O. Fraser
Will Bruce

60 UNDATED DEVOTIONS

CONTENTS

EDITOR'S FOREWORD

This book combines the writings of four mighty men of God. Each shares insights from a life given to prayer and each reveals a heart for the lost. In order to make this already popular book more widely useful, it has been rearranged to make it possible to use it as a devotional. Since J. Hudson Taylor's writings were already in devotional format, they have been dispersed throughout the book, one brief reflection at the end of each section. Besides using Hudson Taylor's *When You Pray* devotional, we have also been able to add portions from five other of his works, *Dwelling In Him, Fruit Bearing, God's Fellow Workers, God's Guiding Hand* and *Great Is Thy Faithfulness.*

In order to keep this book helpful for those who do not want to use it as a devotional, the three sections by Sanders, Fraser and Bruce have been kept in their original order. I believe this is the best possible order as it moves the reader from Insight (Sanders) to Experience (Fraser) to Application (Bruce).

Whether you decide to use this as a devotional or just read it through as you would any book, I believe you will want to keep it on hand with your Bible after you are done and use it for years to come.

FOREWORD

Prayer puzzles most of us. We find it very difficult to define. Stop and think for a moment about how you would define it, and you will see how hard it is. Part of the mystery is that God is neither ignorant, unwilling nor impotent, and therefore he does not need us to intercede on behalf of other men. He knows not only their needs, but also what is best for them. Yet at the same time he teaches us to pray.

The popular idea of prayer is that it is a means of making God do what we want done. This may be a crude and somewhat pagan concept, but it is by no means dead in Christian circles. The natural man has an inbuilt understanding of God, and his concept of prayer is based on the thought of God being hostile or friendly according to how he is treated. If man fulfils certain conditions, he expects God to treat him in a friendly way and to conform his circumstances or those of others to his own desires. Man's nature is basically unchanged: it centres everything around himself. The fact that prayer is a spiritual exercise by no means excludes self-interest and self-centredness. What we want done may even be what we conceive to be God's work, and yet it may still be based on our desires rather on his will. Self-centredness dies hard.

As I have studied the nature of prayer in the New Testament, it seems to me that there are two related aspects of it which affect each other very much. First of all comes prayer that is related to our own concept and personal relationship to God. Worship, adoration, praise, confession and communion all come under this heading. For instance, our worship and the form it takes depend very much on what we think of God and how we are related to him. The second aspect is related to getting something done that affects our circumstances or the lives and circumstances of others. Supplication and thanksgiving come under this heading. The whole purpose of supplication, from our point of view, is that God might so intervene, as either to alter circumstances in some way, or alter the person's reaction to these circumstances. When this happens, we thank God for answering prayer.

The more I study the New Testament, the more I am convinced that the effectiveness of the second kind of praying flows out of the depth of reality in the first kind of praying. Our intercession is directly related to our worship of and communion with God. This means that the effectiveness of our intercession is directly related to our own spiritual life in relation to God and to our own personal prayer life.

When we look at the life of the Lord, we find these related aspects of prayer perfectly balanced. Indeed, intercession without a close relationship to God himself and a daily walk with him can degenerate into mere words.

Without a prayer-cultivated relationship with God we are liable to be doing our own work in our own way and asking God to help and bless, and that fundamentally is an un-Christian way of looking at God and prayer. Prayer is the means of aligning our will with the will of God, of so communing with him that we not only know what he wants done but are also open to guidance and responsiveness in obedience, even at considerable cost.

We learn best by doing. Prayer is no exception to the rule. Prayer is always the first step in involvement, but rarely the last, for prayer brings us into close contact with the will of God and primarily is intended to bring our wills into line with his. That is why prayer is ultimately so practical. God's concern covers the whole wide world, not just our part of it, nor even that other part in which we may have a particular interest. Prayer for all God's people identifies our outlook with his, for God loves the world. Russia, China, South America, Europe and Africa claim prayers of God's people as urgently as anywhere else. Their battle is ours too.

Denis Lane
Former OMF Overseas Director

INTRODUCTION

Prayer is a paradox. No spiritual exercise is such a blend of the complex and the simple. It is the simplest form of speech infant lips can try yet the most sublime strains that reach the Majesty on high. It is as appropriate to the aged philosopher as to the little child. It is the outburst of a moment and the attitude of a lifetime. It is the expression of the rest of faith and of the fight of faith. It is an agony and an ecstasy. It is submissive and yet importunate. In the same moment it lays hold of God and binds the devil. It can be focused on a single objective and it can roam the world. It can be abject confession and rapt adoration. It invests puny man with a sort of omnipotence. Small wonder, then, that even its greatest exponent and example was forced to admit, 'We do not know what we ought to pray for.' But he was swift to add, 'The Spirit himself intercedes for us with groans that words cannot express. And he who searches our hearts knows the mind of the Spirit, *because the Spirit intercedes for the saints in accordance with God's will.*' (Romans 8:26–27, emphasis added).

Our Lord left us in no doubt of the part prayer was to play in the missionary enterprise. He clearly placed it on a prayer basis in the memorable words: 'The harvest is plentiful but the workers are few. *Ask the Lord of the harvest, therefore,* to send out workers into his harvest field' (Matthew 9:37–38). Paul and Barnabas set out on the first missionary journey to the accompaniment of prayer and fasting (see Acts 13:2–4). Ever since, the missionary cause has advanced upon its knees. Where prayer has been lukewarm, it has languished.

Isn't it strange that in spite of our conviction of the privilege and necessity of praying, we are all plagued with a subtle aversion to it? We do not naturally delight in drawing near to God. We pay lip-service to its value and potency and yet so often fail to pray. 'When I go to pray,' confessed one eminent Christian, 'I find my heart is so loath to go to God, and when it is with him so loath to stay.' It is here that self-discipline comes in. 'When thou feelest most indisposed to pray,' counseled an old divine, 'yield not to it. But strive and endeavor to pray even when thou thinkest thou canst not pray.' Here is an area in which we can avail ourselves of the Spirit's promised assistance in our weakness.

Intercessory prayer will take time, but could hours be more strategically spent? Time is a commodity of which there seems to be a universal and chronic shortage. Lack of time is a much overworked excuse for neglect of duty. And yet, strangely enough, even in the midst of an exacting routine we always manage to find time for all we urgently want to do. In reality, the fundamental problem lies not in the time factor, but in the realm of will and desire. We each have all the time there is, and we each choose our own priorities. We automatically place first that which we consider most important. If prayer is meagre it is because we consider it supplemental, not fundamental. To our Lord it was not a reluctant addendum, but a fundamental necessity. The time we spend in prayer will depend on the way we allocate our priorities. If we share Christ's view of the indispensability of prayer, we will somehow make time for it.

That prayer in one aspect is spiritual warfare is clearly taught in Scripture. 'Put on the full armour of God so that you can take your stand against the devil's schemes. For our struggle is not against flesh and blood, but against the rulers, against the authorities, against the powers of this dark world and against the spiritual forces of evil in the heavenly realms. And pray in the Spirit on all occasions with all kinds of prayers and requests. With this in mind, be alert and always keep on praying for all the saints' (Ephesians 6:11–12, 18). In this aspect of prayer, three and not two are involved. Between God and the devil, the god of this world, stands the praying man. Though pitifully weak in himself, he occupies a strategic role in this truceless warfare. His power and authority as he battles in faith are not inherent, but are his through his union with the Victor of Calvary.

Throughout the Gospels, Jesus is seen occupied not so much with the wicked men and evil conditions he confronted, as with the forces of evil behind them. In the words of well-meaning Peter, in the treachery of the traitorous Judas, Jesus detected the black hand of Satan. 'Get behind me, Satan,' he said to Peter (Matthew 16:23). Behind the hideous idol the missionary sees the foul spirit which enslaves the devotee. We see souls bound in sin, but our concern in prayer should be not only to pray for *them*, but also to pray *against Satan* who holds them captive. He must be made to relax his hold on them, and only the power of Christ's victory, appropriated and applied through the prayer of faith, can achieve this. Jesus dealt with the cause, not the effect, and if we are to pray effectively we must follow the same pattern.

In a graphic illustration our Lord likened Satan to a well-armed strong man who kept his palace in peace. Before he could be dislodged and his captives liberated, Jesus said he must first be bound. Only then could the rescue be effected (see Matthew 12:28–29; Luke 11:21–22). 'We may be spiritual and prayerful, courageous and determined,' writes Arthur Wallis, 'we may even succeed in breaking into the strong man's house, but if we have not learned the secret of prayer warfare and how to bind the strong man, he will very likely return in fury and drive us out. Such a counter-attack can have a devastating effect on those who have been praying and labouring hopefully, and it can also supply opposers with the ammunition they require.'

What does it mean to 'bind the strong man,' if not to restrain his activity by appealing to the conquering power of him who was manifested to destroy – render inoperative, powerless – the works of the devil? (See 1 John 3:8). And how can this be done but by the prayer of faith, which lays hold of the victory of Calvary and believes for its manifestation in the situation on which prayer is being focused? Let us not reverse the Lord's order – 'first bind ... then spoil' – and still expect to effect the rescue without neutralising the Adversary. Let us confidently accept our divine-given authority and exercise it. 'I have given you authority ... to overcome all the power of the enemy' (Luke 10:19). Of what value is this delegation of authority if the authority is not exercised?

'Satan dreads nothing but prayer', wrote Samuel Chadwick. 'His one concern is to keep the saints from praying. He fears nothing from prayerless studies, prayerless work, prayerless religion. He laughs at our toil, mocks our wisdom, but trembles when we pray.'

In the history of OMF International, the tide in many a crisis has turned when its workers have met the situation with prayer and fasting. Many a stubborn city has opened, many an intransigent heart has yielded, many a financial need has been supplied and many a delicate personal difficulty has been resolved by this means. While fasting is always optional in the New Testament, the record indicates that it was resorted to in the face of special temptation (see Matthew 4:2); where there was a yearning after a closer walk with God (see 1 Corinthians 7:5); where there was deep concern for evangelising the regions beyond (see Acts 13:1–3); where there was spiritual travail for the development of a church (see Acts 14:21–23); and where some stubborn situation had yielded to no other method (see Matthew 17:21). There is still a place for prayer and fasting, though not on legalistic grounds.

The thumbnail studies in this booklet suggest some of the principles underlying effective prayer, and illustrate these principles from the lives of praying men and women of Bible times. They are presented in this form in the hope that they may prove meaningful and helpful in the hour of prayer.

J. Oswald Sanders

EFFECTIVE PRAYER
J. Oswald Sanders

'God ... calls things that are not as though they were.' Romans 4:17

'Have faith in God.' Mark 11:22

It appears that God acted on the principle of faith in the creation of the world. When he said to non-existent light, 'Let there be light,' there was light. It is this same kind of creative faith we are called on to exercise, the very faith of God. 'Now faith is being sure of what we hope for and certain of what we do not see' (Hebrews 11:1), and this conception opens to us a limited realm of possibility.

The noted scientist Dr. Alexis Carrel writes: 'Prayer is a force as real as terrestrial gravity ... it is the only power in the world that seems to overcome the so-called laws of nature.' In prayer, God places in our hands a kind of omnipotence, enabling us to overcome even unchangeable natural law. Hear the affirmation of the Master, 'Therefore, I tell you, whatever you ask for in prayer, believe you have received it and it will be yours' (Mark 11:24). And if that is not enough to kindle expectation and stimulate faith, consider this: 'If two of you on earth agree about anything you ask for, it will be done for you by my Father in heaven' (Matthew 18:19).

Strangely enough, the human heart is so beset by unbelief that these staggering and all-inclusive promises – 'whatever,' 'anything' – instead of stimulating our faith tend to paralyse it. The mind busily sets to work to conjure up reasons why these universal words can't mean exactly what they say. But they *do* mean exactly what they say.

Unbelief has always shackled omnipotence. Faith releases its might. And faith is not credulity, it is confidence. It rests its weight on the divine guarantee of the infallible Word. It joyously believes that to the God who 'calls things that are not as though they were', nothing is impossible.

REFLECTION

'Faith is being sure of what we hope for.' Hebrews 11:1

'Faith is the substance of things hoped for,' and not mere shadow. It is not less than sight, but more. Sight only shows the outward forms of things; faith gives the substance. You can rest on substance, feed on substance. Christ dwelling in the heart by faith is power indeed.

DAY 2

'Pray continually.' 1 Thessalonians 5:17

Was this exhortation to the Christians at Thessalonica merely a counsel of perfection? Did Paul really consider it an attainable ideal to 'pray in the Spirit on all occasions with all kinds of prayers and requests'? (Ephesians 6:18).

Undoubtedly to him this was both a glorious possibility and an actual experience. 'I remember you in my prayers at all times,' he wrote (Romans 1:10). 'Night and day we pray most earnestly' (1 Thessalonians 3:10). 'Pray the Spirit on all occasions' (Ephesians 6:18). 'Be always on the watch and pray' (Luke 21:36). On God's side, Paul's experience of unceasing prayer sprang from the working of the Spirit of prayer within him. His own part was the response of a sensitive and willing spirit. Nor did he limit himself to formal seasons of prayer. Those informal, involuntary, bursts of prayer native to the praying heart were normal for him. Charles H. Spurgeon once said that for years he had not known a half-hour in which he had not consciously prayed. To him, through disciplined habit, unceasing prayer had become almost instinctive to him, as natural as breathing. To the Spirit-indwelt heart every occurrence, every occasion, becomes the inspiration of prayer.

But prayer is not an exercise of the conscious mind alone. Henry Moorhouse, the great evangelist of a past generation, frequently prayed aloud in his sleep. 'I sleep, but my heart waketh' (see Song of Songs 5:2, KJV), was true of him. Even in sleep, the ever-burning fire of the Holy Spirit within caused the fragrant incense of prayer to ascend from the altar of his heart.

It is our privilege to form this blessed habit, to find in God a friend always within call, to use everything as an occasion for prayer. Through intimacy and obedience we may know the Holy Spirit's unceasing intercession within us (see Romans 8:27), just as on high our great high priest never ceases interceding for us (see Hebrews 7:25).

REFLECTION

'We will give ... our attention to prayer.' Acts 6:4

Shall we not, each one of us, determine to labour more in prayer and cultivate more intimate communion with God by his help, thinking less of what we do and more of what he does? Then he will in actual deed be glorified in and through us!

'Have faith in God.' Mark 11:22

'It is easy to become a fatalist in regard to prayer. It is easier to see unanswered prayer as the will of God than to deliberately reason out the causes of defeat.' But should we be less honest in our approach to this perplexing problem than a merchant to his adverse balance sheet? Perhaps our reluctance to analyse our failures in prayer is rooted in a mistaken concern for God's honour. God is more honoured when we ruthlessly face our failure and diligently search for its cause than when we piously ignore it.

The underlying reason for every unanswered prayer is that in some way we have asked amiss (see James 4:3). Could it be we have substituted faith in prayer for faith in God? Nowhere are we exhorted to have faith in *prayer*, but we are counselled: 'Have faith in God' (Mark 11:22). Faced with this problem the disciples asked 'Why couldn't we?' 'Because you have so little faith', the master replied (see Matthew 17:19–20). An analysis of our prayers might bring about the disconcerting discovery that many are not the prayer of faith at all, only the prayer of hope, or even of despair. We earnestly hope they will be answered, but have no unshakable assurance that they will. However, God has agreed to answer only the prayer of faith. 'Whatever you ask for in prayer, believe that you have received it, and it will be yours' (Mark 11:24). Don't think the translator got his tenses wrong! It is we who have got our attitude wrong!

Another prolific cause of defeat in the prayer life is a secret sympathy with sin. 'If I regard' – cling to – 'iniquity in my heart, the Lord will not hear me.' So let us search out and correct the causes of our unanswered petitions.

REFLECTION

'How will he not ... graciously give us all things?' Romans 8:32

We never have to wait for God's giving. God has already 'blessed us with all spiritual blessings in heavenly places in Christ.' We may reverently say, he has nothing more to give for he has given his all. Yet we may be unable to receive all he has given if the self-life is filling to some extent our hearts and lives.

'I have given you authority ... to overcome all the power of the enemy.' Luke 10:19

The missionary is engaged in a spiritual warfare against intangible and spiritual foes. For such a conflict only spiritual weapons are adequate, but they are 'mighty through God to the pulling down of strongholds' 2 Corinthians 10:4, KJV). Of these the most potent is the weapon of 'all prayer' (Ephesians 6:18), and it can be wielded by others on the missionary's behalf.

To his seventy eager disciples the Lord to whom 'all authority in heaven and on earth' had been given (Matthew 28:18) said, 'I have given you authority ... to overcome all the power of the enemy' (Luke 10:19). With this affirmation, he linked, 'I saw Satan fall like lightning from heaven.' The unmistakable inference was that, through exercising their delegated authority, they too would see the overthrow of Satan in their sphere of responsibility. Nor were they disappointed. 'Lord, even the demons submit to us in your name', the radiant missionaries reported (Luke 10:17).

This promised authority was not withdrawn, but when they lost vital faith in Christ's promise his disciples were powerless to deliver a demon-possessed boy (see Matthew 17:19). They were paralysed by their own unbelief. After his resurrection the Master once again affirmed their privilege. 'In my name' – my authority – 'they will drive out demons' (Mark 16:17).

In this way, we have been given this same spiritual authority today over Satan's power, to be exercised through prayer. Christ, by his death and victorious resurrection, has 'destroyed' – rendered powerless – the devil. As members of his body, united by a living faith, we may participate in his victory, not only for ourselves, but on behalf of those in distant lands. His triumph becomes ours. As we pray, making use of Christ's authority so clearly delegated to us, we can be instrumental in binding 'the strong man' in any given situation. The missionary can then 'spoil his goods'.

REFLECTION

'If you have faith as small as a mustard seed ...' Matthew 17:20

Though your faith were small as a grain of mustard seed it would be enough to move mountains. We need a faith that rests on a great God, and that expects him to keep his own word and to do just as he has promised.

DAY 5 Praying for Missionaries

'You help us by your prayers.'
2 Corinthians 1:11

'Join me in my struggle by praying to God *for* me' the great missionary apostle pleaded (Romans 15:30). In spite of his great gifts of nature and of grace, we search in vain for any sign of conscious adequacy. 'Who is equal to such a task?' Paul asks (2 Corinthians 2:16). Small wonder if his weaker successors crave the intercession of God's people. But what shall we ask God for them?

A veteran missionary facing the fierce opposition of the Adversary in the South Seas wrote, 'There is nothing more profitable, more priceless, that you can ask for us than that in spite of physical weariness, frequent infirmities and the care of multiplying converts, we may be enabled to remain on our knees. For there is a praying in detail to be done if the infant churches are to grow and prosper.' This is a key subject for intercession. Our prayers can make the prayers of our missionary friends especially potent and prevailing.

Note in these verses the juxtaposition of the hard-pressed missionary's extremity and his deliverance. 'We were under great pressure, far beyond our ability to endure ... but [God] has delivered us from such a deadly peril ... as you help us by your prayers' (2 Corinthians 1:8–11). Our intercession may be instrumental in delivering missionaries from 'wicked and evil men' (2 Thessalonians 3:2). Closed doors can be made to swing open on their unwilling hinges as we lay hold of God (Col. 4:2).

Though preaching presented no difficulty to Paul, he entreated the Ephesians, 'Pray also for me, that whenever I open my mouth, words may be given me so that I will fearlessly make known the mystery of the gospel' (Ephesians 6:19).

Joshua prevailed in the conflict in the valley only while Moses' hands were raised to heaven. When they grew slack and fell, Amalek prevailed. We can have the strategic upholding ministry of Aaron and Hur.

REFLECTION

'God's fellow workers.'
2 Corinthians 6:1

I so want you to realise this principle of working with God and asking him for everything. If the work is at the command of God, then we can go to him in full confidence for workers; and when God gives the workers, we can go to him for means to supply their needs.

'My Father will give you whatever you ask in my name. He will give it to you.'
John 16:23

How tame and insipid is much modern praying – a respectable request for a minimum expenditure and exhibition of divine power. Seldom do our petitions rise above the level of natural thought or previous experience. Do we ever dare to pray for the unprecedented? The whole atmosphere of the age tends to make us minimize what we can expect of God. Yet his Word reveals that the extent of legitimate expectation is literally without limits.

As though to anticipate our reluctance to ask audaciously, God employs every universal term in our language in his promises to the praying soul. Here they are: Whatever, wherever, whenever, whoever, all, any, every. Take one such promise. 'My Father will give you whatever you ask in my name' (John 16:23). Trace the other words in their relation to prayer and note how they encourage large petitions. It has been said that God's only limitation and condition of prayer is found in the character of the one who prays – 'According to your faith will it be done to you' (Matthew 9:29).

God delights to respond to daring prayer. How quickly he responded to the audacity of the Syrophoenician woman though she had no right to claim an answer. He encourages us to ask as freely for the impossible as for the possible. To him all difficulties are the same size – less than himself. Because this was so Jesus said, 'If you have faith as small as a mustard seed, you can say to this mountain, "Move from here to there" and it will move. Nothing will be impossible for you' (Matthew 17:20). In the parallel passage, it is a tree and not a mighty mountain. But audacious prayer is no more dismayed by a mountain than a tree, since 'everything is possible for him who believes' (Mark 9:23).

REFLECTION

'He who promised is faithful.'
Hebrews 10:23

If any of you were offered a Bank of England note, whether for five pounds or for five thousand pounds, you would never doubt the value of it. You would take the words printed on it as sure. And are not the words printed in this book (the Bible), as sure? No part of the book is unworthy of our belief. It is either God's word or it is not.

'But the church was earnestly praying to God ...' Acts 12:5

The fact that unity gives birth to strength is a principle of grace as well as of nature. A number of Christians uniting in prayer for a given person or objective brings special power into operation. Their unison demonstrates that oneness which God delights to see and acknowledge (John 17:11). Both scripture and contemporary experience indicate there is a cumulative power in united praying. Faith is infectious, and infection spreads where numbers congregate. Unbelief thrives more readily in isolation. A fire can be kindled with a single stick only with great difficulty.

Our Lord suggested the intensification of prayer force in united praying when he said, 'If two of you on earth agree about anything you ask for, it will be done for you' (Matthew 18:19). At a united prayer meeting the mighty power of Pentecost was unleashed (see Acts 2:1–2). When the believers 'raised their voices together in prayer to God' the place was shaken (Acts 4:24, 31). The prayer of the whole church secured Peter's release (see Acts 12:5). The missionary enterprise had its birth in a united prayer meeting of church leaders (see Acts 13:1–4).

The effective fervent prayer of a righteous man can accomplish much. But scripture and experience combine to teach that the united prayers of many righteous accomplish still more.

REFLECTION

'They all joined together constantly in prayer.' Acts 1:14

Not many days after this, in answer to united and continued prayer, the Holy Spirit did come upon them, and they were all filled ... since the days before Pentecost, has the whole church ever put aside every other work, and waited on God for ten days, that that power might be manifested? We have given too much attention to method and to machinery and to resources, and too little to the source of power.

'They should always pray and not give up.' Luke 18:1

Our Lord taught his disciples by contrast as well as by comparison. Contrary to what may superficially appear to be the teaching of two parables recorded in Luke's Gospel, God is neither a cranky neighbour unwilling to get up to grant our requests (see Luke 11:5), nor is he a greedy judge dispensing reluctant justice (see Luke 18:7). He is illustrating one of the secrets of prevailing prayer. If an ungenerous neighbour can in the end be coerced by his friend's shameless persistence (the very word used) into granting his request, how much more will their heavenly Father give them what they need? If an unjust judge can be badgered into giving justice to a wronged widow simply because he is wearied to death with her appeals, how much more will God respond to the urgent cries of his children?

Half-hearted asking comes away empty-handed. Lukewarmness in prayer, as in everything else, is revolting to God. Shameless persistence, an urgency that will not be denied, returns with the desired favour in its hands. Shameless asking brought the petitioning friend as many loaves as he needed. His first 'asking' met with curt refusal. Then he began to 'seek', to implore his neighbour's help in his distress, only to be denied again. At last he resorted to 'knocking' and hammered at the door until insistence triumphed over obstinate refusal. The same shameless persistence secured for the widow the vindication and compensation she had so long and vainly sought.

That 'they should always pray and not give up' was our Lord's word to the disciples. God may not always give at our first asking. He may have something important to teach us as we 'cry out to him day and night' (Luke 18:7). We may need to 'seek' and 'knock' as well as 'ask'. But he is not impatient with our constant coming, and he will respond to our importunity.

REFLECTION

'He asked this only to test him.' John 6:6

Difficulties are sure to increase, but the power of the Lord is unlimited. When he asks you or me where we shall buy bread, or how we shall solve this or that problem, it is only to prove us. He always knows what he will do; and if we wait his time, he will show us also.

Strenuous Praying

'Join me in my struggle by praying to God for me.' Romans 15:30

'All vital praying makes a drain upon a man's vitality. True intercession is a sacrifice, a bleeding sacrifice, a perpetuation of Calvary, a filling up of the sufferings of Christ.' Such was the conviction of Dr. J. H. Jowett. Jesus worked many mighty works without outward sign of strain, but he offered up prayers and supplications with 'loud cries and tears' (Hebrews 5:7). Our Lord's intercession was a costly ministry for him. It will be the same for the one who follows in his train.

Intercession is no dreamy reverie accompanied by a warm glow of pleasing emotion. Instead it is depicted as 'wrestling', 'agonising'. 'Epaphras ... is always wrestling in prayer for you' (Colossians 4:12). Our 'agonise' derives from the word used here. How pale a reflection of Epaphras' intercessions are our languid prayers!

The same word is used of a man toiling at his work until thoroughly weary (see Colossians 1:29), or striving in the arena for the coveted prize (see 1 Corinthians 9:25). It describes the soldier fighting for his life on the battlefield (see 1 Timothy 6:12), or the man who struggles to defend his friend from danger (see John 18:36). It pictures the agony of earnestness of a man to save his own soul (see Luke 13:24). But its supreme significance appears in the tragedy of Gethsemane. 'Being in anguish, he prayed more earnestly' (Luke 22:44). It was an anguish induced by his identification with and grief over the sins of a lost world.

True intercession is costly. Our Lord first gave himself, then interceded for his murderers. He could do no more for them. 'Are we asking God for something we could supply ourselves? Can it be intercession until we are empty handed? True intercession demands the sacrifice and dedication of all.' Have we given ourselves, have we given all we can for those we intercede for, or are our prayers costless and crossless?

REFLECTION

'If it dies, it produces many seeds.'
John 12:24

Fruit-bearing involved cross-bearing. 'Except a corn of wheat falls into the ground and die, it abideth alone'. We know how the Lord Jesus became fruitful – not just by bearing his cross, but by dying on it. Do we know much fellowship with him in this?

DAY 10   Prayer and the Promises

'For no matter how many promises God has made, they are "Yes" in Christ. And so through him the "Amen" is spoken by us to the glory of God.'
2 Corinthians 1:20

Apromise by God is a pledge by God. It provides the guarantee and forms the basis of the prayer of faith. The stability of a promise rests on the character and resources of the one who makes it, in the same way the value of a check depends on the probity and resources of the one who signs it. The character and fidelity of God vouch for the credibility of the promises he makes.

It is entirely with such promises that the prayer of faith is concerned. As we claim a promise of the word of God, the Holy Spirit imparts the faith to believe that its terms will be fulfilled in the context of our prayer. With God, promise and performance are inseparable.

But promises must be distinguished from facts. We accept a stated fact of God's word, but we plead a promise. When God proclaims a fact, faith accepts and acts on it. When God makes a promise, we comply with its conditions, claim its fulfilment and receive the promised favour. The function of the prayer of faith is to turn God's promises into facts of experience.

The patriarchs obtained the fulfilment of God's promises through faith (see Hebrews 11:33), and turned them into personal experience.

The prayer of faith is neither based on outward circumstances nor on inward feelings. The prayer of faith finds its greatest opportunity when sight brings no helpful vision and comfortable emotions are largely absent. It springs from the naked promise or affirmation of the word of God. It proceeds only from a divine guarantee. The prayer of faith is the power which converts promise into performance.

'The weapons we fight with ... have divine power to demolish strongholds.'
2 Corinthians 10:4

Prayer is not pious daydreaming; it is spiritual warfare. 'For our struggle is not against flesh and blood' Paul says (Ephesians 6:12). Then what is it? It is conflict 'against the rulers, against the authorities, against the powers of this dark world and against the spiritual forces of evil in the heavenly realms' (Ephesians 6:12). But what an unequal contest! What a frightening prospect to someone conscious of his own weakness! Yet it is to such a conflict we have been committed.

What is the divine strategy? The fulcrum on which the battle turns is our ability to pray the right way. It is a spiritual as well as a military maxim that the best defence is attack. Our Commander's plan is for his church to constantly attack on all fronts. Nowhere does he envision a church on the defensive. It is to press the battle to the very gates of hell, and they 'will not overcome it' (Matthew 16:18). The devil's last line of defence is unable to withstand that victorious assault.

What is our weapon? Our Leader has placed in our hands the irresistible sword of the Spirit which defeated the devil in the wilderness – the word of God. But its aggressive and conquering power is released only through the prayer of faith. Our instructions are, 'Take the sword of the Spirit ... pray in the Spirit on all occasions with all kinds of prayers and requests ... and always keep on praying for all the saints' (Ephesians 6:17–18). This is no mere passive praying. Only aggressive prayer based on the word of God dislodges the enemy from his citadel. For 'the weapons we fight with ... have divine power to demolish strongholds' (2 Corinthians 10:4). Such praying releases all the resources of God and brings them into use on the field of battle. Costly? Yes, but also conquering!

REFLECTION

'Be ... faithful in prayer.'
Romans 12:12

Don't be disheartened if you meet with difficulties. All things are working together for good, as we shall see in due time. Pray much. Satan is a terrible reality, so is the flesh; but greater is he who is within us. If God be with us, who can overcome us?

DAY 12   Abraham – Logic in Prayer

'Abraham approached him and said: "Will you sweep away the righteous with the wicked?"' Genesis 18:23

The processes of prayer and answer are not irrational. In fact, God encourages argument in prayer. While he requires submission to his revealed will, he is not pleased with languid passivity. '"Present your case," says the LORD, "Set forth your arguments"' (Isaiah 41:21). We are invited to muster and present the strongest possible arguments for our petition and to press it with logic and vigour.

Confronted with the imminent doom of Sodom, home of his nephew Lot, Abraham, one of the great praying men of the Bible, does just this. His first recourse is prayer to the God with whom he enjoyed such unique intimacy that they actually shared secrets (see Genesis 18:17). In the intensity of his desire, Abraham mixes audacity with argument and petition with pleading. Observe his holy daring as he intercedes. Note his growing confidence as he organizes his appeals. 'Will you sweep away the righteous with the wicked? ... Far be it from you to do such a thing ... will not the Judge of all the earth do right?' (vv.23–25). He argues that such action would compromise God's moral character and tarnish his honour. As God graciously responds, Abraham returns time and again with larger demands, tempering his boldness with suitable reverence.

'I am nothing but dust and ashes ... May the Lord not be angry' (vv.27–30). He ceases his suit upon reaching what he undoubtedly considered the smallest possible number of righteous people in Sodom.

His optimism proved unwarranted. He stopped pleading before he exhausted the mercy and grace of God, and therefore was unable to save Sodom from its doom. Nevertheless, his intercession snatched his nephew from the very jaws of death, for '[God] remembered Abraham, and he brought Lot out of the catastrophe' (Genesis 19:29).

REFLECTION

'Find rest, O my soul, in God alone.'
Psalm 62:5

To most of God's children there come times of sudden awakening when some unexpected trial, illness or bereavement reveals, with startling effect, how, all unconsciously perhaps, our souls were not waiting 'only upon God', but were leaning on an instrument, or on circumstances. Surely, surely, he should not be our last resource, but the first to whom we turn in our difficulties, whether small or great.

'His hands remained steady till sunset.'
Exodus 17:12

'The Amalekites came and attacked ... so Joshua fought the Amalekites.' Between these cryptic sentences stands a third. 'I will stand on top of the hill with the staff of God in my hands' (Exodus 17:8–10). Here is a pictorial presentation of God's missionary strategy – chosen men interlocked with the foe, a chosen man exercising his authority in prayer. No possible connection is apparent between these isolated men, yet their functions were inextricably linked. In the fluctuations of battle the key to final victory was in the hands, not of the fighters on the field, but of the intercessor on the mount.

Prayer is more potent than armies. It was the weapon-less hand of prayer that controlled the issues of battle. 'As long as Moses held up his hands, the Israelites were winning, but whenever he lowered his hands, the Amalekites were winning' (v.11).

Holding our hands high in prayer can be exhausting work. As the tides of battle ebbed and flowed, 'Moses' hands grew tired' (v. 12). The inactivity of praying on the mount is a much greater test of spiritual stamina than battling in the valley. When Moses could no longer stand, he sat. When he could no longer raise his hands, he summoned help. He must not fail Joshua in the valley. At whatever cost, the staff of God must be held aloft.

Joshua must fight as though there was no uplifted staff on the mountain. Moses must pray as if there was no drawn sword in the valley. 'Which things are an allegory' (Galatians 4:2, KJV). Divinely chosen warriors are battling satanic powers in distant lands. The final issue lies in the hands of distant intercessors who have been entrusted with divine authority (see Luke 11:10). Only as their hands are 'steady till sunset' (v. 12) will Amalek be utterly destroyed.

REFLECTION

'I want to know Christ.'
Philippians 3:10

Oh, to know him! How good, how great, how glorious – our God and Father, our God and Saviour, our God and sanctifier: to know him! Pray on and labour on. Don't be afraid of the toil; don't be afraid of the cross; they will pay well.

'Do not be afraid, Daniel ... your words were heard ... but the prince of the Persian kingdom resisted me ...'
Daniel 10:12–13

Elijah was a brilliant meteor in Israel's firmament, whereas Daniel was a fixed star. For over seventy years, and through five reigns as prime minister of mighty Babylon, he wielded a prodigious influence. The divine record compresses his secret into four words: 'He kneeled ... as aforetime' – a three times per daily spiritual exercise (Daniel 6:10, KJV). The tyrant king could not compel him to bow to his golden image. The jealous courtiers could not keep him on his feet when the appointed hour for prayer arrived.

Ezekiel selected Daniel as one of the great intercessors of Old Testament times (see Ezekiel 14:14). It was his praying which broke the chains of the Babylonian captivity, setting Israel free to fulfil the divine purpose. But it was no desultory and sporadic prayer. It took seventy years of faithful intercession before he witnessed Israel's emancipation. Nor was his praying uncontested. His visible enemies endeavoured to keep him from the act of prayer. His invisible adversaries opposed the answering of his prayer. 'The prince of the Persian kingdom resisted me twenty-one days' (Daniel 10:13).

Daniel learned that invisible forces rule the world, that the course of global events can be influenced by the persistent praying of one man. Once the angel Gabriel came to him while in the act of prayer (9:21). Now it was Michael who became his ally against his unseen foe (10:13), assuring him that his prayer was heard from the very moment it was uttered, though the answer was delayed for three weeks.

Prayer is often a contest between angels who minister and demons who hinder. Prayer unanswered is not always prayer denied. Sometimes it is prayer delayed through invisible spiritual activity. It was Daniel's continued wrestling on earth while the battle raged in the heavenlies, that finalised the victory.

REFLECTION

'Hold on to what you have until I come.'
Revelation 2:25

I believe we shall see those successful who can abide God's time with patience. If the storm comes, let us bow to it, but hold on to our anchor. If we cannot make much headway, let us try to hold on, and in time, wind and tide will change. God may try us; he will not fail us.

'Subject to like passions as we are, and he prayed earnestly ...' James 5:17, KJV

God's man for the hour is the man who has mastered the prayer of faith. Because of his prayers, Elijah flamed like a meteor across the midnight of Israel's apostasy. Man of like passions with us, he was a man of unlike passion in prayer. He threw all the fiery forces of his nature into his praying (see James 5:17). Before ever he crashed on to the stage of Israel's history, he had graduated in the school of prayer. He was no novice in the art of taking hold of God. Only long intimacy with the Almighty could give birth to such audacious prayers of faith.

Who else had the serene faith to expect God to stop the beneficent course of nature at his word (James 5:17)? Who else had offered a prayer that rent the sky with heaven's vindicating flame (1 Kings 18:38)? His prayers had prevailed in private before he put God to the test in public. His faith created the atmosphere in which God could work his miracles. Because he stood consciously before God he could stand fearlessly before the king (1 Kings 18:15). The divine response to his prayer of faith demonstrated to the nation that God was God, and brought them on their faces in awe before Him (v.39).

Elijah's faith had the divine promise of rain on which to rest (v.1). But he had no promise of fire. Yet so well did he know his God that he dared to commit him so that he could not fail to respond without compromising his own character and existence (vv.36–37). His prayers invaded a realm never before challenged – the domain of death (17:21–22). When he prayed for rain, he did not require the comforting assurance of sight (v.43). He could believe God without any evidence to the senses. This is the prayer of faith.

REFLECTION

'Able to do immeasurably more than all we ask or imagine.'
Ephesians 3:20

If we claimed all the promises, and asked with all the presumption of loved and favoured children above and beyond all the promises, he would still be able to do exceedingly abundantly above all we ask or think. He delights to do so!

'Oh, that you would bless me and enlarge my territory.' 1 Chronicles 4:10

There is an ambition in prayer which is well-pleasing to God. He is not honoured by the presenting of minimum requests. Because we are coming to the throne of a great king, we should honour him by bringing worthy petitions. Granting them will not strain his resources.

Jabez is an example of ambitious praying which merits our emulation. That his praying met the conditions of divine approval is affirmed by the divine response: 'And God granted his request' (1 Chronicles 4:10). In spite of the hereditary handicap hinted at in his name (Sorrowful) his prayer life lifted him far above the level of his contemporaries. 'Jabez was more honourable than his brothers' (v.9). From the graveyard of the dead whose names are recorded in these opening chapters, he alone is singled out for honourable mention. It was his prayer which gained him this fame.

His intensity of aspiration is shown in its opening clause – the vocative plea of Holy Scriptures. He would not be content with any ordinary blessing from the hand of God. He appealed for an extension of his boundaries. He was not 'content to fill a little space' for God when he could fill a great one. The unselfishness and purity of his motives is guaranteed by the answer granted. Ambition of this kind prevents our spiritual stature from shrinking.

With true realism he asked that God's hand be with him to equip him for larger responsibilities. Because enlarged territory inevitably attracted increased attention on the part of his enemies, he pleaded for God's surrounding and protecting presence. His prayer came before the prayer of our Lord, 'Protect them from the evil one' (John 17:15). God is still looking for men and women whose ambition expresses itself in a prayer like that of Jabez.

REFLECTION

'He is the faithful God, keeping his covenant.'
Deuteronomy 7:9

God has been faithful to us, as far as we have gone out on his promises and have trusted his faithfulness; but how little we have done so! How small, after all, have been our prayers and expectations, seeing we have such a God to do with.

'Hezekiah ... spread it out before the Lord.' Isaiah 37:14

Simplicity is not necessarily stupidity. A man may be childlike without being childish. Indeed, faith is always characterized by simplicity. Hezekiah, king, soldier and poet, was artless in his relationship with God. Rabshakeh and his overwhelming hosts surrounded the royal city. He used every trick to shake the morale of the people. When confronted with a taunting and blasphemous letter from Rabshakeh, Hezekiah's spontaneous reaction was to commit the matter to his God. 'He went up to the temple of the Lord and spread it out before the Lord' (Isaiah 37:14). Behold the simplicity of faith! As though God could not read the letter when rolled up! But his was a simplicity which moved the heart and hand of God. Hear the sequel. 'Then the angel of the Lord went out and put to death a hundred and eighty five thousand men in the Assyrian camp' (v.36). Mighty armies are defenceless before the feeble breath of prayer. Hezekiah's enemies were destroyed not by his military might or strategy but by his simple prayer.

To ask God to reconsider and revoke his decree presented no insuperable problem to this man of simple heart.

When Isaiah communicated to him God's edict that he would die, his faith was not staggered. As was his habit, he turned to God in prayer (38:2-3). And in response to his prayer God changed his mind!

Think of the height to which his prayer soared. Not only did he have no promise of healing as a basis for his faith, but he had the decree of God that he should die. In spite of this he pressed his plea, and God responded magnificently. After this experience, we need never doubt the power of prayer to move the hand of God. The man who knows God may even reverently challenge his decrees.

REFLECTION

'He fulfils the desires of those who fear him; he hears their cry and saves them.' Psalm 145:19

He knew the desire of my heart, and simply trusting like a child, I brought everything to him in prayer. Thus I experienced, quite early, how he is willing to help and strengthen and to fulfil the desire of those who fear him.

'Hannah was praying in her heart.'
1 Samuel 1:13

Strong, spiritual leaders usually have strong praying mothers. It is not mere coincidence that Bible history frequently records the ancestry of its great men. Praying Samuels come from praying Hannahs. Indeed, Samuel was the direct creation of his mother's wordless praying. 'The Lord remembered her. So in the course of time Hannah conceived and gave birth to a son. She named him Samuel, saying, "Because I asked the Lord for him"' (1 Samuel 1:19–20).

The traditional shame of her childlessness was crushing her spirit. Her rival, Elkanah's other wife, 'kept provoking her in order to irritate her' (v.6). Tried beyond endurance, she repaired to the temple and there poured out her soul to a listening God. The aging priest, Eli, dozing on his seat 'observed her mouth. Hannah was praying in her heart, and her lips were moving but her voice was not heard' (vv.12–13). Eli mistook her inarticulate grief for maudlin intoxication. 'How long will you keep on getting drunk?' he chided her (v.14). She protested that her trouble was grief of heart. She was beside herself with the intensity of her supplication, a prototype of those for whom 'the Spirit himself intercedes

for us with groans that words cannot express' (Romans 8:26). Some prayers affect us too deeply for formal speech.

Hannah accompanied her prayer with a vow. 'If you will … remember … I will give' (1 Samuel 1:11). She kept her promise, and as soon as Samuel was weaned, she presented him to the Lord for life. Then, they worshiped the Lord there (1:28). But now it is not wordless praying. Fervent, passionate words flow out of her heart in an uncontrollable tide of adoration (2:1–10). It was a rhapsody worthy of those of Miriam and Deborah and Mary. Small wonder that Samuel's early years, spent in the company of his praying mother, made him a man with a ministry bathed in prayer.

REFLECTION

'Ask for whatever you want me to give you.' 1 Kings 3:5

Now let's stop and ask ourselves; what do we desire? And then let us claim the promise at once. Have we loved ones unsaved? Have we difficulties to conquer? Have we mountains to remove? Then let us take it to the Lord in prayer.

'The king said to me, "What is it you want?" Then I prayed ...' Nehemiah 2:4

True patriot that he was, Nehemiah's heart was deeply distressed at the desolation of his beloved Zion. Like all other spiritual men he turned his heart burden into prayer. 'For some days I mourned and fasted and prayed ...' (Nehemiah 1:4). And what a model prayer it was, combining adoration, confession, argument and petition (vv.5–11). The sheer impossibility of his desire being granted – leave of absence from the side of a despotic Eastern tyrant for four months – did not daunt his faith. He was sure of his God.

God can never resist faith. As Nehemiah prayed, God worked in the king's heart and suddenly the prayed-for opportunity came (2:1–6). Between the despot's unexpected question and Nehemiah's daring request, he found time for bursts of spontaneous prayer. 'Then I prayed to the God of heaven' (2:4). Not only was he granted leave to go to Jerusalem, but he received full provision for the expedition as well. Once again prayer had invaded the realm of the impossible.

His plan of campaign for the restoration of the city wall was simple. 'Then I prayed ... so we rebuilt the wall' (2:4, 4:6). He prayed as he worked and worked as he prayed. Did enemies mock and hinder? He utters a spontaneous prayer and keeps on building (4:4–6). Did they threaten attack? 'We prayed to our God and posted a guard ...' (4:9). Prayer was no substitute for earnest effort and careful preparation, and work was no hindrance to prayer. He did not reserve his prayers for special occasions, they pervaded all his activities. He worked no mighty miracle. He saw no spectacular vision. But the prayer of his burdened, believing heart secured dramatic results. In fifty-two short days he was able to exult, 'So the wall was completed' (6:15).

Let us practice spontaneous prayer.

REFLECTION

'I prayed to the God of heaven ... we continued the work.' Nehemiah 2:4, 4:21

You can work without praying, but it is a bad plan; but you cannot pray in earnest without working. Do not be so busy with work for Christ that you have no strength left for praying. True prayer requires strength.

'He is always wrestling in prayer for you.' Colossians 4:12

Epaphras, Paul's fellow prisoner, cherished an intense concern for the Christians of his native Colosse and of the neighbouring Lycus valley. 'I vouch for him,' Paul wrote, 'that he is working hard for you' (Colossians 4:13). Epaphras was one of them, a fellow citizen. But the warmth of close natural ties passed over into the passion of spiritual concern. 'He is always wrestling in prayer for you'.

Prison walls could not restrain the flight and freedom of the soul of this spiritual giant. Denied personal contact with his loved flock, he could still exercise the most potent of all ministries on their behalf. His concern for their spiritual advancement expressed itself in agonising prayer. That is the very word used. And it was a reflection of his Lord's Gethsemane travail. No mere passive and benevolent desire! He took it seriously. So real was his identification with his children in the faith that it became a matter of life and death. The picture is of a perspiring wrestler straining every muscle, summoning every last ounce of strength as he contends in the games. Epaphras prayed to the point of exhaustion. Indeed, it became almost an obsession: *'Always wrestling for you'* (emphasis added).

His prayers were not concerned with the trivial. As he prayed, his soul soared in aspiration for his friends. He prayed for their constancy, that without wavering, they would stand firm in the face of seduction and opposition. This was not easily attained in a licentious pagan city. He pleaded for their spiritual maturity that they might go on to perfection, standing perfect and complete. He asked that they might have spiritual discernment and conviction, that they 'may stand firm in all the will of God' (4:12).

It was Epaphras' kneeling which kept the Colossians standing.

REFLECTION

'Every willing man skilled in any craft will help you in all the work.'
1 Chronicles 28:21

How are we to get the beautiful combination of willing, skilful men for the work of God? They are promised to our loyal Master. They must be sought from him. They must be claimed by faith and prayer, as Christ himself directed his disciples to pray to the Lord of the harvest to thrust forth labourers into his own harvest.

'Are there not twelve hours of daylight?'
John 11:9

Which of us has not experienced the difficulty of insufficient time for prayer? At least we tend to excuse ourselves by saying we do not have sufficient time. The late Dr. J. H. Jowett was not sympathetic to such an excuse. 'I think one of the common phrases of our day,' he wrote, 'is the one by which we express our permanent lack of time. We repeat it so often that by the very repetition we have deceived ourselves into believing it. It is never the supremely busy men who have no time. So compact and systematic is the regulation of their day that, whenever you make a demand on them, they seem able to find additional corners to offer for unselfish service. I confess, as a minister, that the men to whom I most hopefully look for additional service are the busiest men.'

Let us face the fact squarely and without excuse – each of us has as much time as anyone else in the world. As in the parable of the pounds, we have each been entrusted with the same amount of time, but not all use it in such a way that we produce a tenfold return. True, we do not all have the same capacity, but that fact is recognised in the parable, and the reward for the servant with the smaller capacity but equal faithfulness is the same. We are not responsible for our capacity. We are responsible for the

strategic investment of our time. If we consider prayer as a high priority, we will so arrange our day to make time for it. When we have comparatively little to carry in our case it seems as full as when we have a lot, because the less we have the more carelessly we pack it. The man who claims to have no time is most likely guilty of 'careless packing'.

What practical steps can be taken to safeguard the securing of sufficient time for prayer?

Stop Leaks. Do not consider your day only in terms of hours, but in smaller areas of time. If we look after the minutes, the hours will look after themselves. Few men packed more into a lifetime than Dr. F. B. Meyer. Of him it was said that like John Wesley he divided his life into spaces of five minutes, and tried to make each one count for God. You would expect this to create intolerable strain. But not with Dr. Meyer. According to his biographer, 'his calm manner was not the sleep of an inactive mind, it was more like the sleep of a spinning top.' Just a little while before his departure he said to a friend, 'I think I am an example of what the Lord can do with a man who concentrates on doing one thing at one time.' The secret of Charles Darwin's achievements, it is said, was that he knew the difference between ten minutes and a quarter of an hour.

D. E. Hoste, successor to Hudson Taylor, in a life acknowledged to be extremely full, always made time for a deep and full prayer life. He gave prayer priority in his life because he considered it most important. But he did not arrive immediately at the mastery of his time. 'It is easy to waste time', he wrote.

'The missionary after breakfast may sit down to read the newspaper, or let time slip by in another way. But this cannot be done in business life. I have found the need of much watchfulness and self-discipline in this matter during my years in the interior. A sensitive conscience about the use of time needs to be maintained.'

Study Priorities. Much time which is not actually wasted, is spent on things of only secondary importance. A fool has been described as a man who has missed the proportion of things. Some of us have the unfortunate habit of being so engrossed in the secondary that we have no time left for the primary. We give such undue attention to petty details that matters of major importance are squeezed out. This is especially the case where prayer is concerned, and our adversary will do all in his power to aid and abet. Check to see whether the essentially spiritual is receiving adequate time, or whether the best is being relegated to a secondary place by that which is good.

Our Lord indicated that the secret of successful living was to sacrifice the pearl of inferior value for the pearl of surpassing worth. Are you doing the most important things, or do you procrastinate, substituting the secondary which makes less stringent demands on you? Weigh carefully the respective values of the opportunities and responsibilities which claim your attention. Omit altogether, or give a very minor place to things of little importance. John Wesley used to say, 'Never be unemployed, and never be triflingly employed.'

The Impelling Motive. To effect a radical change in our use of time so as to make more time for prayer will require strength of purpose and a deep dependence on the Lord's enabling. Not all of us naturally possess inflexible wills. But our wills can be reinforced. We can and should be strengthened with power through his Spirit in our inner being, according to the word' (Ephesians 3:16).

The use of time depends largely on the pressure of motive. Are there motives compelling enough to enable us to change the pattern of our lives, to counter long-indulged habits of laxity in the use of time? Henry Martyn found it impossible to waste an hour in his translation work because of the vision he had of nations waiting for the truth locked up in the book he was translating. The need of a lost world proved an impelling motive to redeem the hours. The driving force in the life of our Lord was revealed in one of his incidental sayings, 'I always do what pleases him' (John 8:29). And for Him there were always twenty-four hours in the day. There might not always be time to eat, but always he made time to pray. There will always be time for everything that is within the will of God.

REFLECTION

'Search me, O God, and know my heart.'
Psalm 139:23

Let us ask him to search us and remove all that hinders his work in us in larger measures. If our Bibles or secret prayer have been neglected, let us confess the evil before God and claim his promised forgiveness, carefully avoiding such occasions of weakness for the future.

THE PRAYER OF FAITH
James O. Fraser

Prayer Determination

The first missionary to the Lisu people of the Upper Salween was going through a deep testing. It was not the privation, nor the loneliness of this isolated outpost, nor the rigors of scaling the steep mountain walls to find tribal settlements, nor even the difficulty of making himself at home with these utterly primitive folk – no, none of these things troubled him. But the lack of abiding fruit in the hearts of the Lisu people – this was his constant burden. 'Give me Lisu converts,' he cried from the heart, 'and I can truly say I will be happy even in a pigsty.'

From Fraser's journal:

January 1. Must watch against getting up too late these intensely cold mornings. The indwelling Christ is my successful weapon against all sin these days – praise him!

January 2. An earnest desire to save souls is on me, but prayer is rather unstable. I must regain my equilibrium in the prayer life. I must maintain, also, my abiding in Christ by prayer without ceasing (silent), which I am now finding blessedly possible. Romans 6 is not now my weapon so much as John 15.

January 4. Finished Finney's autobiography; much help received from it. Finney's strong point is the using of means to an end. My own leading is ... along that line also. I do not intend to be one of those who bemoan little results

while 'resting in the faithfulness of God'. My cue is to take hold of the faithfulness of God and use the means necessary to secure big results.

January 16. Not a single person at service in the morning ... The walls of Jericho fell down 'by faith'. Of all the instances of faith in Hebrews 11, this corresponds most nearly to my case. But not faith only was necessary; the wall fell down after it had been compassed about for seven days. Seven days' patience was required, and diligent compassing of the city every day – which seems to typify encompassing the situation by regular, systematic prayer. Here then we see God's way of success in our work, whatever it may be – a trinity of prayer, faith and patience.

January 18. Prayer, today, rather on general than particular lines; patience the chief thought. Abraham was called out by God and went in blind faith. When he got to the land of promise, he found nothing but a famine – much like me with the Lisu these two years. But Abraham, or his seed, later on possessed the milk and honey of the whole land. God's time had come for Abraham but not for the Amorites. God's time has come for me, but not perhaps, just this month or this year, for the Lisu.

Am impressed, too, that I do not yet know the channels which the grace of God is going to cut out among the people here. Hence general prayer has its place, until God's plan is revealed a little more fully.

There had been a few souls who had professed Christ, but in temptation had fallen back into the ways of their old life. Fraser was brought more and more to a keen realisation of the forces arrayed against him, and also of his need for believers in the homeland who would cooperate with him in prayer.

February 4. No meal till 2 p.m. Thoroughly depressed about state of work at Tantsah. Feel much inclined to 'let Ephraim alone', but I am torn between two alternatives, for I seem to have no leading to leave Tantsah. My prayer is not so much, 'Lord lead me somewhere else', as, 'Lord, give me a solid church here at Tantsah.'

February 5. I am not taking the black, despondent view I took yesterday. The opposition will not be overcome by reasoning or by pleading, but (chiefly) by steady, persistent prayer. The men need not be dealt with (it is a heartbreaking job, trying to deal with a Lisu possessed by a spirit of fear) but the powers of darkness need to be fought. I am now setting my face like a flint: if the work seems to fail, then pray; if services etc., fall flat, then pray still more; if months slip by with little or no result, then pray still more and get others to help you.

March 13. Cloud seems to have lifted considerably – perhaps because prayer

burden fought right through ... After much pressure, even agony, in prayer for Lisu souls, enabled to break through into liberty, and to pray the definite prayer of faith for signal blessing among the Lisu during the next few months ... Real, prevailing prayer, for the first time for a week or more, and well worth the travail that led up to it ... Much peace and rest of soul after making that definite prayer, and almost ecstatic joy to think of the Lisu Christian families I am going to get.

August 27. The cross is going to hurt – let it hurt! I am going to work hard and pray hard too, by God's grace.

REFLECTION

'If a man remains in me and I in him, he will bear much fruit.'
John 15:5

It is unbelief that saps our strength and makes everything look dark; and yet he reigns, and we are one with him, and he is making everything happen for the very best. So we ought to always rejoice in him, and rest, though it is not always easy. We must triumph with God, and then we shall succeed with men, and be made blessings to them.

DAY 23 Prayer Cooperation

Can it be that a great work for God involving thousands of souls devolves upon our prayer life – half a world away?

Work on Our Knees. I am feeling more and more that it is, after all, just the prayers of God's people that call down blessing on the work, whether they are directly engaged in it or not. Paul may plant and Apollos water, but it is God who gives the increase; and this increase can be brought down from heaven by believing prayer, whether offered in China or in England. We are, as it were, God's agents – used by him to do his work, not ours. We do our part, and then can only look to him, with others, for his blessing. If this is so, then Christians at home can do as much for foreign missions as those actually on the field. I believe it will only be known on the last day how much has been accomplished in missionary work by the prayers of earnest believers at home. And this, surely, is the heart of the problem. Such work does not consist in curio exhibitions, lantern lectures, interesting reports, and so on. Good as they may be, these are only the fringe, not the root of the matter. Solid, lasting missionary work is done on our knees. What I covet more than anything else, is earnest, believing prayer, and I write to ask you to continue in prayer for me and [for] the work here.

When the Tide Comes In. I cannot insist too strongly on my own helplessness among these people apart from the grace of God. Although I have been now 10 years in China and have had considerable experience with both Chinese and Lisu, I find myself able to do little or nothing apart from God's going before me and working among men.

Without this I feel like a man who has his boat grounded in shallow water. Pull or push as he may, he will not be able to make his boat move more than a few inches. But let the tide come in and lift his boat off the bottom – then he will be able to move it as far as he pleases, quite easily and without friction. It is indeed necessary for me to go around among our Lisu preaching, teaching, exhorting, rebuking, but the amount of progress made thereby depends almost entirely on the state of the spiritual tide in the village – a condition which you can control upon your knees as well as I can.

A Volume of Faith. Praying without faith is like trying to cut with a blunt knife – much labour expended to little purpose. For the work accomplished by labour in prayer depends on our faith: 'According to your faith be it unto you' (Matthew 9:29).

I have been impressed lately with the thought that people fail in praying the prayer of faith because they do not believe that God has already answered, but only that he will some time or other answer their petitions. This is not the faith that makes prayer effective. True faith glories in the present tense, and does not trouble itself about the future. God's promises are in the present tense and are quite secure enough to set our hearts at rest. Their full outworking is often in the future, but God's word is as good as his bond and we need have no anxiety. Sometimes he gives at once what we ask, but more often he just gives his promise (see Mark 11:24). Perhaps he is more glorified in this latter case, for it means that our faith is tried and strengthened. I do earnestly covet a volume of prayer for my Lisu work – but oh! For a volume of faith too. Will you give this?

REFLECTION

'*Everything is possible for him who believes.*' Mark 9:23

People say, 'Lord, increase our faith.' Did not the Lord rebuke his disciples for that prayer? He said, 'You do not want a great faith, but faith in a great God. If your faith were as small as a grain of mustard seed, it would suffice to remove this mountain!'

'I am an engineer and believe in things working. I want to see them work', Fraser used to say. And because he believed that prayer works – 'If ye shall ask ... I will do' (John 14:14) – and that God means it when he guarantees results from energy spent in prayer (James 5:16–18), Fraser determined to provide prayer material for more prayer supporters so that the volume of prayer rising for the Lisu work would constantly increase.

'I know you will never fail me in the matter of intercession', he wrote to his mother, 'but will you think and pray about getting a group of like-minded friends, whether few or many, whether in one place or scattered, to join in the same petitions? If you could form a small prayer circle I would write regularly to the members.'

What a number of earnest, spiritually minded Christians there are at home, *(Fraser wrote on his return to Tengyueh after an arduous survey trip)*, and how correspondingly rich are the prayer forces of the church! How I long for some of this wealth for myself and the Lisu here. I have had it in measure already, but I should very, very much like a wider circle of intercessors.

Our work among the Lisu is not going to be a bed of roses, spiritually. I know enough about Satan to realise that he will have all his weapons ready for determined opposition. He would be a missionary simpleton who expected plain sailing in any work of God. I will not, by God's grace, let anything deter me from going straight ahead in the path to which he leads, but I shall feel greatly strengthened if I know of a definite company of prayers holding me up. I am confident that the Lord is going to do a work, sooner or later, among the Lisu here.

About three years later:

Knowing as I do the conditions of the work, its magnitude (potentially), its difficulties and the opposition it meets with, I have definitely resolved, with God's help, to enlarge the place of my tent, to lengthen my prayer cords and strengthen my intercessory stakes, to make a forward movement with regard to the prayer circle.

I am persuaded that the homeland is rich in godly, quiet, praying people in every denomination. They may not be a great multitude as far as numbers are concerned, but they are 'rich in faith', even if many of them be poor and of humble station. It is the prayers of such that I covet more than gold of Ophir – those good men and women who know what it is to have power with God and prevail. Will you help me, prayerfully and judiciously, to get some of these to join the circle? The work for which I am asking prayer is preaching and teaching the word of God, pure and simple. I have no confidence in anything but the gospel of Calvary to uplift these needy people.

After the work had begun to show the shape of things to come:

The Lisu and Kachin converts would be easily able to support their own pastors, teachers and evangelists by well-advised cultivation of their own ample hillsides, and it is fitting that the mountains should bring forth supplies for the needs of those whose feet are beautiful upon them. But spiritually they are babes, and as dependent upon us as a child upon his mother. They are dependent on us out here for instruction, guidance, organization; but they are dependent on the home churches in England and America in a deeper sense, for spiritual life and power. I really believe that if every particle of prayer put up by the home churches on behalf of the infant churches of the mission field were removed, the latter would be swamped by an incoming flood of the powers of darkness. This seems actually to have happened in church history – churches losing all their power and life, becoming a mere empty name, or else flickering out altogether. Just as a plant may die for lack of watering, so may a genuine work of God die and rot for lack of prayer.

One might compare heathenism with a great mountain threatening to crush the infant church, or a great pool of stagnant water always threatening to quench the flames of Holy Ghost life and power in the native churches, and only kept dammed up by the power of God. God is able to do this and much more, but he will not do it if all of us out here and you at home sit in our easy chairs with arms folded. Why prayer is so indispensable we cannot say, but we had better recognise the fact even if we cannot explain it. Do you believe that the church of God would be alive today were it not for the high priestly intercession of the Lord Jesus Christ on the throne? I do not: I believe it would have been dead and buried long ago. Viewing the Bible as a record of God's work on this earth, I believe that it gives a clear, ringing message to his people – from Genesis to Revelation – you must do your part.

The church of Protestant countries is well able to nourish the infant church of the Orient by a steady and powerful volume of intercessory prayer. Applying this to the work among the Tengyueh tribespeople, I feel I can say that you, and those God will yet call to join you in this prayer work, are well able to sustain the spiritual life of the Lisu and Kachin converts, as well as to increase their number many-fold. It may be he has been preparing you for the unseen and spiritual parenthood of these infant Lisu converts here, however many thousand miles separate you from them.

I am not asking you just to give 'help' in prayer as a sort of sideline, but I am trying to roll the main responsibility of this prayer warfare on you. I want you to take the burden of these people upon your shoulders. I want you to wrestle with God for them. I do not want so much to be a regimental commander in this matter as an intelligence officer. I shall feel more and more that a big responsibility rests upon me to keep you well informed. The Lord Jesus looks down from heaven and sees these poor, degraded, neglected tribespeople. 'The travail of his soul' was for them, too. He has waited long. Will you not do your part to bring in the day when he shall 'be satisfied'?

Anything must be done rather than let this prayer service be dropped or even allowed to stagnate. We often speak of intercessory work as being of vital importance. I want to prove that I believe this in actual fact by giving my first and best energies to it, as God may lead. I feel like a businessman who perceives that a certain line of goods pays better than any other in his store, and who purposes making it his chief investment; who, in fact sees an inexhaustible supply and an almost unlimited demand for a profitable article and intends to go in for it more than for anything else. The demand is the lost state of these tens of thousands of Lisu and Kachin – their ignorance, their superstition, their sinfulness; their bodies, their minds, their souls; the supply is the grace of God to meet this need – to be brought down to them by the persevering prayers of a considerable company of God's people. All I want to do is, as a kind of middleman, to bring the supply and the demand together.

REFLECTION

'If you believe, you will receive whatever you ask for in prayer.' Matthew 21:22

Seeing that in days of old, faith wrought such mighty wonders ... and that we have the same God ... shall we not ask great things? Believing prayer will lead to wholehearted action, and the Lord for our encouragement says, 'If two of you shall agree on earth as touching anything that they shall ask, it shall be done for them of My Father which is in heaven'.

It was his own daily contact with the 'darkness that can be felt' in the battle for souls that led Fraser to share with his prayer constituency some thoughts on the heart attitude which leads to effective prayer.

Prepare for Prayer. 'If two of you shall agree' (Matthew 18:19) – I felt, even when praying alone, that there are two concerned in the prayer, God and myself ... I do not think that a petition which misses the mind of God will ever be answered (1 John 5:14). Personally, I feel the need of trusting him to lead me in prayer as well as in other matters. I find it helpful to preface prayer not only by meditation but by the definite request that I be directed into the channels of prayer to which the Holy Spirit is beckoning me. I also find it helpful to make a short list, like notes prepared for a sermon, before every season of prayer. The mind needs to be guided as well as the spirit attuned. I can thus get my thoughts in order, and having prepared my prayer can put the notes on the table or chair before me, kneel down and get to business.

With the Understanding Also. Always remember, 'I will pray with the spirit, and I will pray with the understanding also' (1 Corinthians 14:15). Let the Spirit and the understanding work in about equal proportions. First, think over the needs taking into account any consciousness of spirit-burden. Pray, tentatively, along that line, asking God continually to focus your prayers. If, after covering such ground in prayer, no 'grip' comes anywhere, it is probably best to close down at once. Do not be in a hurry to do this, but don't press on in the energy of the flesh.

Hannah's Prayer. I was very severely disappointed about the attitude of the Lisu of that district [near Tantsah] to the gospel. They received the word with joy at first, as they so often do. Several announced that they were going to turn Christian, and one old man and his son seemed especially earnest. Then the spirit of fear seemed to possess them, and one by one they dropped off until no one would take a stand at all. We had to leave them as heathen as I first found them. It was a very painful experience and seemed almost to stun me for a while.

How much of our prayer is of the quality we find in Hannah's 'bitterness of soul' when she 'prayed unto the Lord' (1 Samuel 1:10)? How many times have we 'wept sore' before the Lord? We have prayed much, perhaps, but our longings have not been deep compared with hers. We may have spent much time on our knees without our hearts going out in an agony of desire. But real supplication is the child of heartfelt desire, and it cannot prevail without it. This is not an earthly desire, nor does it issue from our own sinful hearts, but it is wrought into us by God himself. Oh, for such desires! Oh, for Hannah's earnestness, not in myself only but in all who are joining me in prayer for these poor heathen aborigines!

And is there not sufficient reason for such earnestness? We have our Peninnahs as surely as Hannah had and as God's saints have had all down the ages. David's eyes ran with rivers of water because the ungodly did not observe God's law (Psalm 119:136). Jeremiah wept with bitter lamentation because of the destruction of the holy city. Nehemiah fasted, mourned, and wept when he heard of the fresh calamities which had befallen Jerusalem. Our Lord wept before it because of its hardness of heart. The Apostle Paul had 'great sorrow and unceasing pain' in his heart on account of his brethren according to the flesh (Romans 9:2).

Yes, and we have our 'sore provocations', or should have. How else ought we to feel when we see all the ungodliness and unbelief around us on every hand? Would a light-hearted apathy become us under such circumstances? No, indeed! And I want you, please, to join me – or, rather, share with me – in the 'provocation' which is daily with me in my work among the Lisu. Let the terrible power of evil spirits among them be a provocation to you. Let their sinfulness, their fears, their pitiful weakness and instability be a provocation to you. Ask God to lay the burden upon you, and that heavily – that it may press you down upon your knees. My prayer for you is that God will work such sorrow within you that you will have no alternative but to pray. I want you to be 'sore provoked' as I am.

Such a state of mind and heart is only useful, however, as it is turned into prayer. Desire, however deep, does nothing in itself any more than steam pressure in a boiler is of use unless it is allowed to drive machinery. There is a spiritual law here. A strong spiritual desire does harm rather than good if it is neglected. An earnest desire in spiritual things is a bell ringing for prayer. Not that we should wait for such desires. We should pray at all seasons, whether we are prayer-hungry or not. If we have a healthy prayer-appetite, so much the better. But if this appetite is unnoticed or unappeased, a dullness will come over us and we shall be weakened in spirit, just as lack of sufficient food weakens us in body. See, in 1 Samuel 1:15, the way in which Hannah dealt with her God-given desire. Her soul was bitter, and she 'poured it out' before the Lord.

Blessed bitterness! But it must be poured out.

REFLECTION

'Ask God... and it will be given.' James 1:5

We must all get nearer to God; we must abide in Christ; our lives must be more up to our principles and privileges, and all will be well. Let us trust for all, and we shall find all. God can bless; let us ask it in faith, and expect it. Nothing else, nothing less can satisfy him; nothing less must satisfy us.

DAY 26 The Prayer of Faith - I

The scriptures speak of several kinds of prayer. There is intercession and there is supplication, there is labour in prayer and there is the prayer of faith; all perhaps the same fundamentally, but they present various aspects of this great and wonderful theme. It would not be unprofitable to study the differences between these various scriptural terms.

There is a distinction between general prayer and definite prayer. By definite prayer I mean prayer after the pattern of Matthew 21:21–22 and John 15:7, where a definite petition is offered up and definite faith exercised for its fulfilment. Now faith must be in exercise in the other kinds of prayer also, when we pray for many and varied things without knowing the will of God in every case.

In general prayer I am limited by my ignorance. But this kind of prayer is the duty of us all (1 Timothy 2:1–2), however vague it has to be. I may know very little, in detail, about the object of my prayer, but I can at any rate commend it to God and leave it with him. It is good and right to pray, vaguely, for all people, all lands, all things, at all times.

But definite prayer is a very different matter. It is in a special sense 'the prayer of faith'. A definite request is made in definite faith for a definite answer.

Take the case of a Canadian immigrant as an illustration of the prayer of faith. Allured by the prospect of 'golden grain' he leaves home for the Canadian West. He has a definite object in view. He knows very well what he is going for, and that is wheat. He thinks of the good crops he will reap and of the money they will bring him – much like the child of God who sets out to pray the prayer of faith and who has his definite object too. It may be the conversion of a son or daughter; it may be power in Christian service; it may be guidance in a perplexing situation, or a hundred and one other things – but it is definite. Consider the points of resemblance between the cases of the prospective Canadian farmer and the believing Christian.

The Breadth of the Territory. Think of the unlimited scope for the farmer in Canada. There are literally millions of acres waiting to be cultivated. No need, there, to tread on other people's toes! Room for all – vast tracts of unoccupied land just going to waste, and good land too. And so it is with us, surely. There is a vast, vast field for us to go up and claim in faith. There is enough sin, enough sorrow, enough of the blighting influence of Satan in the world to absorb all our prayer of faith, and a hundred times as many more. 'There remaineth yet very much land to be possessed' (Joshua 13:1).

Government Encourages Immigration. Think also of the efforts the Canadian government is making to encourage immigration. All the unoccupied land belongs to it, but settlers are so badly needed that they are offered every inducement – immigration offices established, sea passages and railway fares reduced, and grants of land made free! God is no less urgently inviting his people to pray the prayer of faith: 'Ask – ask – ask', he is continually saying to us. He offers his inducement too: 'Ask and ye shall receive, that your joy may be full' (John 16:24). All the unoccupied territory of faith belongs to him. And he bids us to come and occupy freely. 'How long are ye slack to go in to possess the land ... ?' (Joshua 18:3).

REFLECTION

'But when he asks, he must believe and not doubt.' James 1:6

A full knowledge of the word will often bring to our recollection appropriate promises, and thus enable us to pray with that faith and confidence which are so closely connected with answers to prayer.

The Prayer of Faith - II

Fixed Limits. Yet this aspect of the truth must not be overemphasised. Though it is a blessed fact that the land is so broad, it can easily be magnified out of due proportion. The important thing is, not the vastness of the territory, but how much of it is actually assigned to us. The Canadian government will make a grant of 160 acres to the farmer-immigrant, and no more. Why no more? Because they know very well he cannot work any more. If they were to give him 160 square miles instead of 160 acres he would not know what to do with it all. So they wisely limit him to an amount of land equal to his resources.

And it is much the same with us when praying the prayer of definite faith. The very word 'definite' means 'with fixed limits'. We are often exhorted, and with reason, to ask great things of God. Yet there is a balance in all things, and we may go too far in this direction. It is possible 'to bite off', even in prayer, 'more than we can chew'. There is a principle underlying 2 Corinthians 10:13, ('We, however, will not boast beyond proper limits, but will confine our boasting to the field God has assigned to us, a field that reaches even to you') which may apply to this very matter. Faith is like muscle which grows stronger and stronger with use, rather than rubber which weakens when it is stretched. Overstrained faith is not pure faith; there is a mixture of the carnal element in it. There is no strain in the 'rest of faith'. It asks for definite blessings as God may lead. It does not hold back through carnal timidity nor press ahead too far through carnal eagerness.

I have definitely asked the Lord for several hundred families of Lisu believers. There are upwards of 2,000 Lisu families in the Tantsah district. It might be said, 'Why do you not ask for 1,000?' I answer quite frankly, 'Because I have not faith for a thousand'. I believe the Lord has given me faith for more than 100 families, but not for 1,000. So I accept the limits the Lord has, I believe, given me. Perhaps God will give me 1,000; perhaps he will lead me to commit myself to this definite prayer of faith later on. This is in accordance with Ephesians 3:20, 'above all we ask or think'. But we must not overload faith; we must be sane and practical. Let us not claim too little in faith, but let us not claim too much either. Remember the Canadian immigrant's 160 acres. Consider, too, how the Dominion government exercises authority in the matter of location. The government has a say as to the where as well as the how much of the immigrant's claim. He may not wander all over the prairie at his own sweet will and elect to settle down in any place he chooses. Even in regard to the position of his farm he must consult the government.

Do we always do this in our prayers and claims? Do we consult the 'heavenly government' at the outset, or do we pray the first thing that comes to mind? Do we spend time waiting upon God to know his will before attempting to embark on his promises? That this is a principle upon which God works he has informed us very plainly in 1 John 5:14–15: 'And this is the confidence that we have in him, that, if we ask any thing according to his will, he heareth us: And if we know that he hears us, whatsoever we ask, we know that we have the petitions that we desired of him.'

I cannot but feel that this is one cause for many unanswered prayers. James 4:3 ('Ye ask, and receive not because ye ask amiss, that ye may consume it upon your lusts.') has a broad application, and we need to search our hearts in its light. Unanswered prayers have taught me to seek the Lord's will instead of my own. I suppose we have most of us had such experiences. We have prayed and prayed and prayed, and no answer has come. The heavens above us have been as brass. Yea, blessed brass, if it has taught us to sink a little more of this ever-present self of ours into the cross of Christ. Sometimes our petition has been such a good one, to all appearances, but that does not ensure its being of God. Many 'good desires' proceed from our uncrucified selves. Scripture and experience certainly agree that those who live nearest to God are the most likely to know his will. We are called to be 'filled with the knowledge of his will' (Colossians 1:9). We need to know more

of the fellowship of Christ's death. We need to feed on the word of God more than we do. We need more holiness, more prayer. We shall not, then, be in such danger of mistaking his will.

It does not follow that because a thing is the will of God, he will necessarily lead you to pray for it. He may have other burdens for you. We must get our prayers from God, and pray to know his will. It may take time. God was dealing with Hudson Taylor for fifteen years before he laid upon him the burden of definite prayer for the foundation of the China Inland Mission. God is not in a hurry. He cannot do things with us until we are trained and ready for them. We may be certain he has further service, further burdens of faith and prayer to give us when we are ready for them.

REFLECTION

'He chose our inheritance for us.'
Psalm 47:4

Having carefully laid our plans and determined to carry them through, we may ask God to help us, and to prosper us in connection with them. Yet another way of working is to begin with God; to ask his plans, and to offer ourselves to him to carry out his purposes. Going about it in this way, we ... have no responsibility save to follow as we are led.

DAY 28
The Prayer of Faith - III

The Claim Endorsed. Turn to the immigrant again. He has come to an agreement with the Canadian government. He falls in with their terms, he accepts their conditions, he agrees to take over the land allotted to him. So he presents his claim at the proper quarter, and it is at once endorsed. Could anything be simpler? Nor need our claim in the presence of God be any less simple. When we once have the deep, calm assurance of his will in the matter, we put in our claim, just as a child before his father. A simple request and nothing more. No cringing, no beseeching, no tears, no wrestling. No second asking either.

In my case I prayed continually for the Tengyueh Lisu for over four years, asking many times that several hundreds of families might be turned to God. This was only general prayer, however. God was dealing with me in the meantime. You know how a child is sometimes rebuked by his parents for asking something in a wrong way – perhaps in the case of a child, for asking rudely. The parent will say, 'Ask me properly'. That is just what God seemed to be saying to me then: 'Ask me properly. You have been asking me to do this for the last four years without ever really believing that I would do it – now ask in faith'.

I felt the burden clearly. I went to my room alone one afternoon and knelt in prayer. I knew that the time had come for the prayer of faith. And then, fully knowing what I was doing and what it might cost me, I definitely committed myself to this petition in faith. I cast my burden upon the Lord and rose from my knees with the deep, restful conviction that I had already received the answer. The transaction was done. And since then (nearly a year ago now) I have never had anything but peace and joy (when in touch with God) in holding to the ground already claimed and taken. I have never repeated the request and never will: there is no need. The asking, the taking, and the receiving occupy but a few moments (Mark 11:24). It is a solemn thing to enter into a faith covenant with God. It is binding on both parties. You lift up your hand to God, you definitely ask for and receive his proffered gift – then do not go back on your faith, even if you live to be 100.

REFLECTION

'The righteous ... are in God's hands.'
Ecclesiastes 9:1

'Let us leave all in the hands of God' ... make it a matter of prayer and then leave it in the hands of God our Father. I have prayed about it, and I am sure I can trust God. He will do all things well. God knows what is best and we must learn to welcome his will, which is good, acceptable and perfect.

Get to Work. To return once more to the Canadian farmer. He has put in his claim, the land has been granted, the deed made out and sealed with the official seal. Is that the end then? No! Only the beginning!

He has not attained his object yet. His object is a harvest of wheat, not a patch of wasteland; and there is a vast difference between the two. The government never promised him sacks of flour all ready for export – only the land which could be made to yield them. Now is the time for him to roll up his sleeves and get to work. He must build his homestead, get his livestock, call in labourers, clear the ground, plough it and sow his seed. The government says to him in effect, 'We have granted your claim – now go and work it.'

And this distinction is no less clear in the spiritual realm. God gives us the ground in answer to the prayer of faith, but not the harvest. That must be worked for in cooperation with him. Faith must be followed up by works, prayer-works. Salvation is of grace, but it must be worked out if it is to become ours (Philippians 2:12). And the prayer of faith is just the same. It is given to us by free grace, but it will never be ours till we follow it up, work it out. Faith and works must never be divorced, for indolence will reap no harvest in the spiritual world. I think the principle will be found to hold in any case where the prayer of faith is offered, but there is no doubt that it always holds good in cases where the strongholds of Satan are attacked, where the prey is to be wrested from the strong.

Think of the children of Israel under Joshua. God had given them the land of Canaan – given it to them, notice, by free grace – but see how they had to fight when once they commenced actually to take possession!

Satan's tactics seem to be as follows. He will first of all oppose our breaking through to the place of real, living faith by all means in his power. He detests the prayer of faith, for it is an authoritative 'notice to quit'. He does not so much mind rambling, carnal prayers, for they do not hurt him much. This is why it is so difficult to attain to a definite faith in God for a definite object. We often have to strive and wrestle in prayer (Ephesians 6:10–12) before we attain this quiet, restful faith. And until we break right through and join hands with God we have not attained to real faith at all. Faith is a gift of God – if we stop short of it we are using mere fleshly energy or willpower, weapons of no value in this warfare. Once we attain to a real faith, however, all the forces of hell are impotent to annul it. What then? They retire and muster their forces on this plot of ground which God has pledged himself to give us, and contest every inch of it. The real battle begins when the prayer of faith has been offered. But, praise the Lord! We are on the winning side. Let us read and re-read the tenth chapter of Joshua, and never talk about defeat again. Defeat, indeed! No. Victory! Victory! Victory!

• Read 2 Samuel 23:8–23. All I have been saying is found in a nutshell in verses 11 and 12, ('Next to him was Shammah son of Agee the Hararite. When the Philistines banded together at a place where there was a field full of lentils, Israel's troops fled from them. But Shammah took his stand in the middle of the field. He defended it and struck the Philistines down, and the Lord brought about a great victory.') Let Shammah represent the Christian warrior. Let David represent the crucified and risen Christ – and note that Shammah was one of the 'mighty men whom David had'. Let the 'plot of ground' represent the prayer of faith. Let the lentils, if you will, represent the poor lost souls of men. Let the Philistines represent the hosts of wickedness. Let 'the people' represent Christians afflicted with spiritual anaemia.

I can imagine what these people were saying as they saw the Philistines approaching and ran away! 'Perhaps it was not the Lord's will to grant us that plot of ground. We must submit to the will of God.'

Yes, we must indeed submit ourselves to God, but we must also 'resist the devil' (James. 4:7). The fact that the enemy comes upon us in force is no proof that we are out of the line of God's will. The constant prefixing of 'if it be thy will' to our prayers is often a mere subterfuge of unbelief. True submission to God is not inconsistent with virility and boldness. Notice what Shammah did – simply held his ground. He was not seeking more worlds to conquer at that moment! He just stood where he was and hit out right and left. Notice also the result of his action and to whom the glory is ascribed!

REFLECTION

'Now do it!'
2 Samuel 3:18

'Try' is a word constantly in the mouth of unbelievers. 'We must do what we can,' they say. It is far too often taken up by believers. In our experience, 'to try' has usually meant 'to fail'. The word of the Lord in reference to his various commands is not, 'Do your best,' but 'Do it'; that is, do the thing commanded.

Praying Through to Victory. I repeat that this does not necessarily apply to every kind of prayer. A young Lisu Christian here is fond of telling an experience of his a few months ago. He was walking through the fields in the evening when his insides began unaccountably to pain him. He dropped on his knees and, bowing his head down to the ground, asked Jesus to cure him. At once the stomach ache left him. Praise the Lord! And there are, no doubt, multitudes of such cases – simple faith and simple answers. But we must not rest content with such prayer. We must get beyond stomach ache or any other ache, and enter into the deeper fellowship of God's purposes. 'That ye be no longer children' (Ephesians 4:14). We must press on to maturity. We must attain to 'the measure of the stature of the fullness of Christ' and not remain in God's kindergarten indefinitely. If we grow into manhood in the spiritual life we shall not escape conflict. As long as Ephesians 6:10–18 remains in the Bible, we must be prepared for serious warfare – 'and having done all, to stand'. We must fight through, and then stand victorious on the battlefield.

Isn't this another secret of many unanswered prayers – that they are not fought through? If the result is not seen as soon as expected, Christians are apt to lose heart, and if it is still longer delayed to abandon it altogether.

We must count the cost before praying the prayer of faith. We must be willing to pay the price. We must mean business. We must set ourselves to see things through 'with all perseverance' (Ephesians 6:18). Our natural strength will fail, and herein lies the necessity for a divinely given faith. We can then rest back in the everlasting arms and renew our strength continually. We can then rest as well as wrestle. In this conflict-prayer, after the definite exercise of faith, there is no need to ask the same thing again and again. It seems to me inconsistent to do so. Under these circumstances, I would say let prayer take the following forms:

a. A firm standing on God-given ground, and a constant assertion of faith and claiming of victory. It is helpful, I find, to repeat passages of scripture applicable to the subject. Let faith be continually strengthened and fed from its proper source – the word of God.

b. A definite fighting and resisting of Satan's host in the name of Christ. I like to read passages of scripture such as 1

John 3:8 or Revelation 12:11 in prayer as direct weapons against Satan. I often find it a means of much added strength and liberty in prayer to fight in this way. Nothing cuts like the word of the living God (Heb. 4:12).

c. Praying through every aspect of the matter in detail. In the case of my Lisu work here I continually pray to God to give me fresh knowledge of his will, more wisdom in dealing with the people, knowledge of how to pray, how to maintain victory, how to instruct the people in the gospel, or in singing or in prayer, help in studying the language, help in ordinary conversation, help in preaching, guidance as to settling down somewhere as a centre, guidance about building a house (if necessary), guidance in my personal affairs (money, food, clothes etc.), help and blessing in my correspondence, openings for the word and blessing in other villages, for leaders and helpers to be raised up for me, for each of the Christians by name, also for every one of my prayer helpers by name. Such detailed prayer is exhausting, but I believe effectual in regard to ascertaining the will of God and obtaining his highest blessing.

REFLECTION

'I have set the Lord always before me.'
Psalm 16:8

Let us see to it that we keep God before our eyes; that we walk in his ways, and seek to please and glorify him in everything, great and small. Depend on it, God's work, done God's way, will never lack God's supplies.

Ten years had passed. The groundwork of prayer, faith and patience was well laid in Lisuland. The steady plodding round and round that Jericho wall continued year after laborious year not only by Fraser himself but also by his faithful prayer forces at home. When would God's time come and the prayer of faith be fulfilled? Should Fraser stay on, waiting and praying, while other more responsive fields lay idle because of lack of harvesters?

The day came when Fraser felt that a time must be set. One more journey around the district from village to village where he was well known; then if the Lord did not indicate otherwise, he would offer for another field for a time – until the time for harvest came among the Lisu. He started out on that 'last' journey. The response was the same dull apathy – or was it? As he set out early the second morning his host, who had been wholly noncommittal the night before, declared that as a family they wanted to turn from their demon worship to God's way. Fraser could scarcely believe his ears. Others followed after this first family had made the break. All during that journey calls came from villages high up on the mountainside, or deep down in the ravine, or across the valley. Not only family after family but village after village made a public decision to turn from darkness to light, from the power

of Satan to God. Was it too good to be true? No! The movement of God so long prayed for was gradually spreading throughout the area. God's time had come.

I believe it was January 12, 1915, that I was definitely led to ask God for 'several hundreds of families' from the Lisu. Some may say, 'Your prayer has at last been answered.' No! I took the answer then. I believed then that I had it. The realisation has only now come, it is true, but God does not keep us waiting for answers. He gives them at once (Daniel 9:23).

I wish you could have been with me as I went from village to village, to have seen the royal reception they gave me! And you would have shared in it too. What with the playing of their bagpipes, the firing off of guns, the lining up of all the villagers, men and women, young and old, to shake hands with you (they use both hands, thinking it more respectful) you have a feeling of being overwhelmed – an 'overweight of joy'.

Imagine what it is to have between 500 and 600 families (representing some 3,000 people) looking to you as father, mother, teacher, shepherd and adviser! It is a big responsibility.

I went in for big things when I took up tribes work and I do not regret it. I believe that to a large extent we get what we go in for with God – only sometimes we have mistaken ideas as to how it will come about. Rejoice with me and pray on for them all, in every phase of need you can think of.

The people are perhaps shivering through their rags. They are poor, dirty, ignorant and superstitious, but they are God's gift to us. You ask God for spiritual children, and he chooses them out for you. You shake hands with the brothers and sisters and mothers he has found for you, and sit down with the boys and girls all around you. For I would rather teach Lisu children to sing 'Jesus loves me, this I know' than teach integral calculus to the most intelligent student who has no interest in China.

Two things stand out clearly in my mind: first, how 'foolish' and 'weak' our new converts are; and second, that God has really chosen them. 1 Corinthians 1:27–28 is fulfilled before my very eyes! If you could come out here and see how useless mere preaching and persuasion is among these people, you would understand this better. One feels so helpless in face of their ignorance and need! But the Lisu work in our present district, with over 200 families on either side of the Salween River (400 and more families in all), has been spontaneous from the beginning.

They will take you to a village you have never set foot in or even heard of before, and you will find several families

of converts there, some of whom can now read and write after a fashion, and a chapel already put up! They just teach one another – inviting converts over from neighbouring villages for that purpose. They just want to be Christians when they hear all about it and turn Christian, missionary or no missionary. Who put that 'want-to' in their hearts? If they are not God's chosen, God's elect, what are they?

I used to think that prayer should have the first place and teaching the second. I now feel it would be truer to give prayer the first, second, and third places, and teaching the fourth.

These people out here are not only ignorant and superstitious – they have a heathen atmosphere about them. One can actually feel it. We are not dealing with an enemy that fires at the head only – that keeps the mind only in ignorance – but with an enemy who uses poison gas attacks which wrap the people round with deadly effect, and yet are impalpable, elusive. What would you think of the folly of the soldier who fired a gun into the gas to kill it or drive it back? Nor would it be of any more avail to teach or preach to the Lisu here while they are held back by these invisible forces. Poisonous gas cannot be dispersed, I suppose, in any other way than by the wind springing up and dispersing it. Man is powerless.

But the breath of God can blow away all those miasmic vapours from the atmosphere of a village, in answer to your prayers. We are not fighting against flesh and blood. You deal with the fundamental issues of this Lisu work when you pray against the principalities, the powers, the world rulers of this darkness, the spiritual hosts of wickedness in the heavenlies (Ephesians 6:12).

I believe that a work of God sometimes goes on behind a particular man or family, village or district before the knowledge of the truth ever reaches them. It is a silent, unsuspected work, not in mind or heart, but in the unseen realm behind these. Then, when the light of the gospel is brought, there is no difficulty, no conflict. It is, then, simply a case of 'Stand still and see the salvation of the Lord' (Exodus 14:13).

This should give us confidence in praying intelligently for those who are far from the gospel light. The longer the preparation, the deeper the work. The deeper the root, the firmer the plant when once it springs above ground. I do not believe that any deep work of God takes root without long preparation somewhere.

On the human side, evangelistic work on the mission field is like a man going about in a dark, damp valley with a lighted match in his hand, seeking to ignite anything ignitable. But things are damp through and through and will not burn, however much he tries. In other cases, God's wind and sunshine have prepared beforehand. The valley is dry in places, and when the lighted match is applied – here a shrub, there a tree, here a few sticks, there a heap of leaves take fire and give light and warmth long after the kindling match and its bearer have passed on. And this is what God wants to see, and what he will inquire of us: little patches of fire burning all over the world.

REFLECTION

'Your fruitfulness comes from me.'
Hosea 14:8

'I am the true vine.' The first two words, 'I am', give us the key to the whole secret of fruitfulness. Not what we are, but what he is; not what we do, but what his life works in and through us is the question of the moment. 'From me is thy fruit found.' He is the true fruit bearer.

PRAYER TOOLS
Will Bruce

Every Christian in our modern world is under constant satanic pressure and attack. We must bear one another's burdens as we see these pressures escalating. We can and must do this by regular, specific prayer. So much of our praying is limited to just, 'Lord, bless ... ' or, 'Lord, meet the need of ... '

We are admonished in Galatians 6:2 to bear one another's burdens. Some burdens are too heavy to be borne alone. This happens because of a sudden flood of problems, a lack of adequate Bible teaching or because of spiritual immaturity. On the other hand, Galatians 6:5 tells us there are burdens for which each one must take responsibility. He must seek God's help and do what he can for himself. In 2 Corinthians 1:8–11, Paul writes of the extreme pressures that can be handled only through the prayers of others.

To be guilty of the sin of prayerlessness is to be guilty of the worst form of practical atheism. It is actually saying we can get along without his help while the evidence is very clear on every hand that we cannot. Could it be that the sin of prayerlessness stems from our unbelief that he is a living God who exercises direct influence on the affairs of men?

Instead of waiting until crisis problems develop which result in panic praying for others, we need to trust God to protect them as we pray Spirit-led, thoughtful, caring prayers before the problems overwhelm them and they are unable to cope. We need to engage in major battles, not just minor skirmishes, moving from surface praying to in-depth praying. We need to pray both defensively and offensively.

Praying for others is vital to our own spiritual growth. If we pray for them at all we often get bogged down with the material or the trivial and do not move on to the spiritual and the eternal. Where are our priorities? Often they are so clouded by humanistic and materialistic philosophies on the one hand and the pressures of the day on the other that we ignore the spiritual almost entirely. Needless to say, we do not cease to intercede for material needs as we learn to pray protectively for spiritual needs and growth. We need to progress beyond, 'Lord, bless John and Mary' and be specific, thus moving from crisis praying to protective praying.

For example: Fred or Jane is unemployed. We pray for a job, as we should, but what is God saying in this circumstance? What are the spiritual lessons to be learned? What are the attitudes, the frustrations, the mental depressions, and the fears? How about the interpersonal relationships within and outside the family? Is God glorified in this time of stress by their actions and reactions? Many times in our very limited intercession for others we pray for deliverance from difficult circumstance, sickness, or accident. We forget to ask that Fred or Jane will take God's more than ample provision and learn the lessons God has for both in this trial. Our concern is not necessarily for the removal of the problem but for victory in it and God's glory. Daniel was not kept out of the lion's den. He was kept in it!

Another example: After six years of seeing the happy marriage of a fine young couple who have been leading the young people's group, we find that they have filed for divorce on grounds of incompatibility. They say, 'We no longer love each other.' We petition God with deep concern for them in this crisis, but have we been praying for them protectively, strategically, specifically and with discernment during their years of married life?

As we recognise the absolute necessity of praying protectively for one another and bearing one another's burdens, we must not excuse ourselves by saying, 'How can I pray for them when they do not tell me their needs?' Others' needs are often similar to our own. As we think of their needs, God's word and his Spirit will lead us in prayer.

REFLECTION

'Therefore I will boast all the more gladly about my weakness.'
2 Corinthians 12:9

Paul was distressed by a burden which he did not have strength to bear, and asked that the burden might be removed. God answered the prayer, not by taking it away, but by showing him the power and the grace to bear it joyfully. Thus that which had been the cause of sorrow and regret now became the occasion of rejoicing and triumph.

Pray that the one for whom we are interceding:

• **Will realize his present exalted position in Christ.** Paul places the utmost importance on the child of God entering into a mature partnership with the Father. This is partially achieved by realising his present exalted position before God in heaven now through the work of the Lord Jesus on the cross. It is only as we acknowledge who we really are in Christ that we can live this new identity. Many believers seem to be ignorant of this. Pray that others will get their true identity and self-worth from who they are in Christ and not from success, failure or what others say or think about them.

• **Will present himself as a living sacrifice.** In Romans 12:1–2 Paul presents the ultimate and totally necessary step of Christian dedication. This is presenting our bodies and all we have and are as a living sacrifice to God. This commitment is not essential to salvation, but no progress will be made in the Christian life without it. Pray that others, like Paul, will cry out, 'Lord, what do you want me to do?' and then do it.

• **Will be filled with the Holy Spirit.** The Lord commands us to be filled (Ephesians 5:18). The filling of the Holy Spirit is not optional equipment for the Christian. Nothing in the spiritual life is accomplished without his power and in-filling. In the measure that we are not Spirit-filled we are self-centred, selfish and carnal. Pray that the believer will allow the Holy Spirit to work daily in his life.

• **Will be regular and systematic in the study of God's word.** It is essential for us to pray specifically that the one we are praying for will take the word of God as his food, guide, companion, only source of information about God and the spiritual life, only authority, and the ultimate fountain of joy in this life (Psalm 119). Pray, too, that as he is in the word he will appropriate it and obey it, let God's word guide him, show him his blind spots and keep him balanced.

REFLECTION

'That man should not think he will receive anything from the Lord.' James 1:7

Only those prayers will be answered which are in harmony with the revealed will of God. Unless the word of God is abiding in us, how can we be sure that our petitions are in harmony with his will?

Pray that the one for whom we are interceding:

• **Will have the mind of Christ.** In 1 Corinthians 2:11–16 the spiritual man is seen as having both the spirit of man and the Spirit of God. Thus we pray for the believer, that having supernatural life in Christ through the indwelling Holy Spirit, he may appropriate the mind of Christ in all matters of life. Pray that he will choose to make Christ-like decisions in regard to priorities, goals and guidance, with sharpened insights so as not to waste time on good things and miss God's best. Pray that he will constantly live with eternity's values in view, an attitude impossible to attain without the realisation that the Christian life is a miracle life from beginning to end (Galatians 3:1–3).

• **Will grow daily in Christian maturity.** Nothing is more tragic than a twenty-year-old infant! Many today are in that spiritual condition after having been saved for a number of years. Pray that the believer will see that after the crisis experience of being born again there is the lifelong process of daily growth in Christ that takes patience, time, discipline and the power of the Holy Spirit (Ephesians 2:10; 4:11–16; Philippians 2:12–13). The mature Christian must have a spirit of forgiveness with no root of bitterness because of any treatment of himself or others. He must learn to handle stress, frustrations and unfulfilled expectations in a Christ-like manner.

• **Will appropriate the full armour of God.** Pray that the believer will have his eyes opened to the dangers of certain satanic attacks and will put on the full armour of God. The armour plus the skilful use of the authority he has in the victorious Christ insures full protection (Ephesians 6:10–18; Colossians 2:1–15). Pray that the one for whom we are praying will fulfil his responsibility as one born for battle, resist temptation and repent promptly of any sin in his life.

• **Will be alert to Satan's strategy.** Pray that the believer will not only be kept from sin but also that he will be aware of the threefold satanic temptations: the lust of the flesh (fulfilling any of our desires outside the will of God) is Satan's effort to get us out of the will of God; the lust of the eyes (coveting that which God does not allow at a particular time or place) is Satan's effort to get us to distrust God; the pride of life (self effort or independence from God) is Satan's effort to destroy our confidence in God (1 John 2:16). Also he must realise that he is incapable of meeting Satan in his own strength. Victory comes only as he takes the victory of Calvary as his own (1 Corinthians 15:57–58). Pray that he will discern between satanic pressure and godly chastening, and remain keenly alert to all satanic deception.

Pray that the one for whom we are interceding:

• **Will not love the world system.** Pray that the child of God will have mental, emotional, doctrinal and moral stability in a day in which the pressures from peer groups, the media, and the world are increasing in their opposition to biblical standards. The believer must know that love of the world is not consistent with loving God (1 John 2:15–17). Pray that he will realise that his love for God is expressed through obedience (John 14:15, 21, 23).

• **Will have a spirit of brokenness and humility.** Pray that the believer's pride will be broken and that he will deal with his sins through repentance and seeking forgiveness. Psalm 51:17 says: 'The sacrifices of God are a broken spirit; a broken and contrite heart, O God, you will not despise.' Pray for willingness to give and take, willingness to change and willingness to see another's viewpoint. Pray that the believer will have an understanding spirit in place of a judgmental one. Pray that instead of looking for someone to blame in various situations he will be willing to say, 'I am sorry' or 'I was wrong.'

• **Will have a servant's heart.** Pray this believer will be convinced of the Lord's desire for him: that he be a servant of God and of his brothers in Christ (Mark 10:44–45).

• **Will build a scriptural family.** Pray that the one for whom you are praying will look neither to the world nor to carnal Christians but to the word of God, and that he will fulfil his God-ordained place as head and spiritual leader of his home. Pray that his wife will be submissive and seek the Lord's approval as did Sarah when she called Abraham, 'Master' (1 Peter 3:6). Pray that as parents they will be firm, yet loving, realising the absolute necessity of being godly models for their children. Pray that the husband and wife will maintain a balance among family, ministry and job responsibilities (Ephesians 5:14–6:4), that all in the family will love each other with *agape* love, seeking the highest good for each other rather than demanding their rights. Pray for those who are single, that they will look to the Lord for his choice of a life partner, or pray that their lives will glorify God as singles.

• **Will become an effective prayer warrior.** Pray that the believer will have a vital and effective prayer life from a clean heart. It is absolutely necessary to keep short accounts with God. 'If I regard iniquity in my heart the Lord will not hear me' (Psalm 66:18). See also 1 John 1:9. Pray that his praying will be biblically based, specific, consistent, steadfast in the Spirit, in faith and with understanding.

DAY 36

Praying for One Another - V

Pray that the one for whom we are interceding:

• **Will know God's hand on him in physical and material things.** Pray that the one you are praying for will have the measure of health that will best glorify God. Pray that when set aside by ill health he will learn the lessons God has for him and draw upon divine resources. Pray also for safety in travel, financial provision in keeping with God's plan for him and proper use of the time and money God entrusts to him.

• **Will engage in prayerful worship.** To truly worship is to truly serve. Pray that the believer will not be on a treadmill of activity, substituting that for time with the Lord in true worship. Pray, too, that he will learn to praise the Lord, that he will give thanks for who he is in Christ, for spiritual growth, and for the fact that 'God is a living God, he has spoken in the Bible; he means what he says, and will do all he has promised' (J. Hudson Taylor).

• **Will be involved in an accountability team.** Pray that he will not be deceived into thinking that he can stand alone and grow spiritually. Pray that he will select a group, or at least one person who is spiritually mature and committed to walking with God, to whom he will be especially accountable and faithful in all areas of his life. Pray that this commitment will be characterised by openness, honesty and teachableness. Pray that above all he will recognise his accountability to God: 'So then, each of us will give an account of himself to God' (Romans 14:12).

• **Will reach out to the unsaved.** Pray that others will love the lost as the Lord Jesus does and will reach out to a lost and dying world with the message of salvation. The Lord loved the unlovely and the destitute; his disciples should do no less. This love will best be communicated to the lost by a sacrificial sharing of the good news of Christ, sharing of themselves, and at times sharing materially with the hungry and needy. Pray that as God reveals his will as to the type and place of service at home or abroad, those who are his own will respond without hesitation.

REFLECTION

'For to me, to live is Christ.' Philippians 1:21

Has Christ become to us such a living, bright reality that no post of duty is tedious, that as his witnesses we can return to the quiet homeside, or to the distant service, with hearts more than glad, more than satisfied, even if stripped of earthly friends and treasures?

DAY 37   Praying for One Another - VI

So then, how do we pray for one another?

• Confess sin and let the blood of Jesus cleanse. Prayer must flow from a cleansed vessel. Psalm 66:18, 'If I had cherished sin in my heart, the Lord would not have listened.'

• Be tied to the mind of Christ so thoroughly that you think his thoughts about his embattled saints.

• Be motivated by love for God and a desire to help others (Hebrews 6:10).

• Pray fervently to be led by the Holy Spirit to the exact needs of the one for whom you are praying.

• Be specific, systematic and steadfast in praying for others.

• Agree in prayer with others, the 'two or three' of Matthew 18:19–20.

• Learn to saturate a situation or problem with prayer.

• Pray with the authority you have in Christ to bind the power of Satan (Matthew 18:18, Mark 3:27).

• Pray the prayer of faith and claim the victory (1 Corinthians 15:57–58).

• Pray for others as you pray for yourself. Any problem you have, others probably have even if in a slightly different form.

• Use a passage of scripture as you pray for others. Here are some suggestions: Ephesians 1:15–23; 3:14–21; Colossians 1:9–12. (Use scripture also in praying for yourself.)

Accept Your Responsibility. May you accept your responsibility of interceding for others by getting down to the real business of praying for them. 'O God, awaken us all to our responsibility to pray for one another so that all Christians may glorify you and fulfil the purpose for which we have been saved!'

REFLECTION

'In the morning, O Lord, you hear my voice.' Psalm 5:3

Do not have your concert first, and then tune your instruments afterwards. Begin the day with the word of God and prayer, and get first of all into harmony with him.

Why do we say: 'Brothers and sisters, pray for us'? There are many reasons, including those listed below. The full-time missionary must have the intercessory missionary (prayer partner) working with him on a regular, systematic basis. We cannot work independently in the salvation, discipling and training of national leaders (2 Corinthians 10:4).

The missionary is invading enemy territory. In most instances, Satan has held uncontested sway for centuries or even millenniums in the countries which we think of as 'foreign mission fields'. As a result, the thinking of the people is twisted, their minds are blinded, and God's truth does not penetrate easily. Satan does not meekly give up his prey; he counter-attacks in all and many times undreamed-of ways. He fights to the last ditch. We are in the midst of a spiritual battle. Intercessory missionaries must see themselves as part of the same team (see 2 Corinthians 10:4).

Pray that souls will be released from Satan's bondage and will put their trust in Christ. Pray that the missionary will recognise the attacks of the adversary and use scriptural weapons in the battle.

The missionary faces many frustrations. There is much to discourage and frustrate the missionary, such as:

• **Language Disparity.** This means that we cannot clearly communicate the message of God's salvation until we have spent months or even years in language study.

• **Customs and Culture.** These are often different, and sometimes conflict with our Western ways of doing things. But we are guests in these countries and must learn to be careful not to offend by thoughtlessly ignoring things that are important to those we have come to reach with the gospel.

• **Unfamiliar Foods.** These can be delicious or unpalatable. We have to subordinate our own tastes and be prepared to eat what is offered if friendly relationships are to be established.

• **Climate.** We who come from temperate zones often have problems adjusting to the tropics: enervating heat coupled with high humidity, typhoons and rainy season deluges.

• **Lack of Privacy.** Many people in other countries live much of their lives in public and expect the missionary to do the same. We must work out a balance.

• **Lack of Results.** We may not set the world on fire as we expected. There must be a constant 'looking to Jesus'.

Pray for the missionary to be graciously flexible and able in very practical ways to obey the injunction of Philippians 4:6 ('Do not be anxious about anything but in everything ... present your requests to God.')

REFLECTION

'In everything ... present your requests to God.'
Philippians 4:6

The Lord's will is that his people should be strong, healthy and happy. Shall we not determine to be 'careful for nothing, but in everything by prayer and supplication with thanksgiving' bring those things that would become burdens or anxieties to God in prayer and live in his perfect peace?

The missionary has need of self-knowledge. It is not long before we are again forced to face up to the fact of our own sinful flesh. We then recognise afresh how human we are! It's rough to learn what we are really like. Pressure will reveal it all too clearly! Here are a few of the revelations the Lord brings to our attention:

• **Pride of Race.** This may be quite unintentional, yet is apparent to the national; pride of 'face' and love of position or 'place' may also be found.

• **Prejudice.** 'My' way and the way 'I' have been taught is viewed as the only right way.

• **Selfishness.** Lack of consideration for others, wanting attention, stubbornness and the inability to see another's viewpoint can all come from this root of self.

• **Lack of Self-discipline.** It is so easy to waste precious time, our own and others', on the mission field. We may also find that we do not have sufficiently defined, measurable goals for the work and insufficiently detailed programs for accomplishing them.

Pray that the missionary will learn to submit his own desires and inclinations to God's Holy Spirit, and then that the fruit of the Spirit will be more and more apparent in the life of the missionary.

Pray that he will understand and appropriate all he has and is in Christ.

The missionary faces loneliness. It is easy to succumb to loneliness in a foreign land when we are surrounded by people of another culture and language. This is true of those who are single and those who are married. We all need to know we are loved and accepted. Loneliness is one of the means the devil uses to discourage and depress us and to cause us to engage in disastrous self-pity. But God has supplied a way of escape! His promise in Hebrews 13:5b, 'Never will I leave you; never will I forsake you', is as true today as it was when he first gave it. What we need to do is to claim it for ourselves and experience the presence of the Lord Jesus Christ in our everyday living.

Pray that the missionary will experience fellowship with God in new and satisfying ways.

The missionary must remember the meaning of being a missionary. It has been in our Bibles all the time, and on the field we really need to learn the truth of Christ's statement in John 6:38: 'I have come down from heaven, not to do my will but to do the will of him who sent me' and Mark 10:45: 'For even the Son of Man did not come to be served, but to serve, and to give his life a ransom for many.' Our mission is to be servants to all. We are God's instruments, to be used as he sees fit. We must learn to work as team members regardless of our training, or talents, or lack of either.

Pray that the missionary will have the humility of Christ as described in Philippians 2:5–8.

The missionary needs stability. In all areas of life we must maintain equilibrium. Spiritually, there must be doctrinal stability through the study of the Bible and its application to our daily living. Mentally, we must learn how to combat Satan's great tool of depression. Emotionally, we need to strike a happy balance between becoming too calloused or too sympathetic.

Pray that in each of these areas the missionary will develop mature stability. Pray that the missionary will get his true identity and self-worth from who he is in Christ and not from success or what others think or say about him.

The missionary's insight needs to be sharpened. We need insight into the heart-needs of those around us, both nationals and fellow missionaries to diagnose and to apply remedies. We need insight into methods of work in order to know what will best accomplish the task. We need insight concerning our priorities and the setting of goals. Once we acquire a working knowledge of the language, we need real wisdom from God to know which opportunities to pursue and which to leave undone.

Pray that the missionary will have a heightened sympathy and insight into the heart-needs of those around him. Pray, too, that he will have insight and heavenly wisdom to know what God would have him undertake, and how God would have him go about it.

The missionary needs good inter-personal relationships. These are all-important if God's work is to go forward unhindered. The oil of the Spirit of God must be operative to insure that we get along well with others: husband/wife, worker/co-worker, worker/director, worker/national Christian, worker/national unbeliever. If relationships become strained we need to be honest and open with each other, show real repentance, and allow God to break our stubborn pride. It is no easier for us to admit we are wrong than for anyone else! Pray that in this important area the missionary will be surrendered to God and sensitive to the prompting of the Holy Spirit.

Pray that he will see his own personal needs. And that couples would love each other with *agape* love, seeking the highest good rather than claiming their rights.

REFLECTION

'Till the Spirit is poured upon us from on high.' Isaiah 32:15

Our God is an almighty Saviour, and my hope is in him. If his Spirit is poured out, evil will be kept in check. If we ask for it, will it not truly be so? Let us pray then, often, for this, that division and discord may not prevail instead of unity and love.

The missionary needs to be filled with the Spirit. The Spirit's gracious fruit must show in our lives or our work will accomplish nothing. Unless we have daily communion with our Lord, the pressure will result in failure and we will finally drop from foreign service. We must keep spiritually fresh if we are to glorify him.

Pray that the missionary will be able to obey the injunction of Ephesians 5:18 ('be filled with the Spirit') and Galatians 5:16,25 ('keep in step with the Spirit'). Pray that he will always keep short account with God (1 John 1:9), be aware of Satan's deceptions and hate all sin.

The missionary may have health problems. Physical health is important, and many workers have been disqualified for service on the grounds of ill health. Common foes are malaria, hepatitis, amoebic dysentery and dengue fever. Excessive fatigue may cause depression or discouragement, with disastrous results in other areas. We need also to be aware of attacks upon our mental health. Our enemy sometimes attacks our minds, leading to mental and emotional problems. Anxiety and worry will soon drain us of all vitality. We need to learn to guard against these with the 'shield of faith'.

Pray that God will keep the missionary in that condition of health that will best glorify him.

The missionary will travel. Travel on the field is very often hazardous, whether by plane, bus, car or on foot. Sometimes as we send up a quick prayer to God, we wonder if anyone else was led to pray at that moment. Pray for safety in travel.

The missionary's children may have needs. Our sons and daughters can be of the greatest blessing and help to us, or may pose a problem. Sometimes decisions made because of our children have a far-reaching effect on our lives or service, and theirs, too. Sadly, children that are loved but not disciplined can adversely affect our work and testimony. We need wisdom to train and teach them in ways well pleasing to God and in full accordance with his word.

Pray for the health of missionary children. Pray that both parents will be godly role models and will do all they can to help their children develop godly self-worth. Pray that parents may have wisdom in providing for their education. Pray that children, as well as parents, will have a good understanding and attitude if separation should become necessary for schooling. Pray especially that the children will not let any bitterness take root because of separation.

REFLECTION

'How much more will your Father in heaven give ... to those who ask Him.'
Luke 11:13

The many blessings enjoyed even by those who know him not are still given and continued by his grace; and how much more may the children of this heavenly Father look to him with confidence, knowing that he will supply their every need in life, in death, and in the world to come!

The missionary needs to constantly show love. Love is required at all times, in all circumstances, for all people. Our human love will not do; it always falls short. Only the love of God which is 'shed abroad' in our hearts by the Holy Spirit, and has the characteristics outlined in 1 Corinthians 13, will suffice.

Pray for the missionary as Paul prayed in Philippians 1:9 (that love 'may abound more and more in knowledge and depth of insight'). Pray that at all times, in all circumstances, with all people, we will take that which God has so fully and freely provided. 'God has given ... take.'

Share the missionary's burden for additional workers, both national and foreign. With untold millions dying untold, and untaught millions dying untaught, plus the population explosion and the closing of doors, we must have more co-workers to gather in the harvest and disciple those who are coming to Christ.

Pray that many more at home and on the foreign field will make 'his last command their first concern'.

Missionaries should maintain their own intercessory life. Missionaries must take time to pray for every aspect of the work in which they are engaged because they are so intimately involved in the local situation. Pray that the missionary will recognise and faithfully fulfil his part in prayer for the work.

How do you pray for missionaries?

• Be specific, systematic and steadfast.

• Agree in prayer with others (see Matthew 18:19–20).

• Practice saturation praying – covering many aspects with many brief requests.

• Pray as for yourself. Any problem you have, the missionary may also have, but it will be magnified by his situation and circumstances.

• Pray with the authority you have in Christ, and bind the strong man (see Matthew 18:18; Mark 3:27).

• Try using a passage of scripture when you are praying for your missionary, such as Ephesians 1:15–23, Colossians 1:9–14, or Ephesians 3:16–21.

'Someone has said: "Better, far better, do less work, if need be, in order that we may pray more; because work done by the rushing torrent of human energy will not save a single soul: whereas work done in vital and unbroken contact with the living God will tell for all eternity." No doubt, we would all heartily agree with this – the trouble, of course, is to actually put it into practice.'

When God calls Christians into ministry, he desires the whole family to be part of his witness in the community they serve. Strong Christian families can endure hardships, overcome difficulties, persevere in the face of discouragements, and be a powerful witness of God's love and grace through their daily lives. Unfortunately, Satan is also aware that one of his most effective strategies in hindering the Lord's work is to destroy the witness of the family by taking advantage of the vulnerability of children.

Missionaries' kids (MKs) are extremely important members of the missionary team although often not recognised as such. Effective, strategic, knowledgeable prayer on their behalf can prevent the significant loss caused by their not adjusting to God's will for them.

Spiritual Life and Maturing. As with every individual, MKs must personally acknowledge Christ as Lord and Saviour. The MKs' number one priority must be to establish their true personal identity in Christ. Only then can they grow and mature in Christ.

Pray that MKs will have a personal relationship to Christ and put him first in their lives, maintain a vital devotional life, and have a thankful attitude, while still not denying difficulties or griefs. Pray that they will be teachable and willing to accept spiritual guidance from parents, dorm parents and others, so that they will grow up secure, well adjusted and having a self-image based on who they are in Christ, able to remind themselves that Christ lives in them, fully assured of their salvation, and not pitying themselves because they are MKs. Like all children, MKs are seeking personal worth and success which is usually found through encouragement from their parents.

Pray that the MKs will recognise the skills they have as valuable; that they will have courage to pursue their interests; that the parents will positively reinforce the children's good behaviour and encourage development of transferable skills; that MKs will at all times keep their priorities in line with the mind and the will of God; and that their self-worth will be based on being children of God and not on human success.

REFLECTION

'We do not know what to do, but our eyes are upon you.' 2 Chronicles 20:12

I myself, for instance, am not specially gifted, and am shy by nature, but my gracious and merciful God and Father inclined himself to me, and when I was weak in faith he strengthened me while I was still young. He taught me in my helplessness to rest on him, and to pray even about little things in which another might have felt able to help himself.

DAY 44 How to Pray for Missionaries' Kids - II

Family Dynamics. Sometimes lack of stability in missionary families can come from: (1) Failure of each family member to appropriate or understand their position in Christ or to be constantly alert to the deceptive attacks of Satan. (2) Long separations. (3) Rootlessness due to frequent moves. (4) Disunity and poor relationships within the family. (5) Failure to feel part of the ministry and consequent resentment when there are necessary separations. (6) A sense of neglect when letter writing is left to only one parent. (7) Failure to balance responsibilities toward ministry and family, resulting in the Missionaries' Kids (MKs) feeling neglected.

Pray that missionary parents will make their children feel a part of their ministry; that parents of MKs will provide the love and attention their children need; that parents will balance ministry and family needs; that the MKs will learn the value of the parents' ministry; and that parents (especially fathers) will spend quality time with each child one-on-one and with the family alone.

Dealing with Losses and Relationships. Due to constant changes and moves MKs may 'lose' friends and have to cultivate new friendships much more often than their peers at home. Some grow reluctant to establish meaningful relationships and withdraw in despair. MKs need a sense of stability. The parents need sensitivity to any potential confusion in their children.

Pray that the MKs will accept the challenge of separation if it is necessary to live away from their parents, and will have courage to face loneliness and fears. Pray that they will know it's okay to cry or be sad or lonely, but that they will be sure of God's promise: 'Never will I leave you; never will I forsake you' (Hebrews 13:5). Pray they will form close, healthy relationships and mutually supportive friendships with both nationals and their peers; that they will be protected from any who would wrongly influence their thinking; that the MKs will find good mentors; and that they will feel free to openly discuss problems, doubts and confusion. Pray that MKs will reach out to others who need friends, too, and that prayer partners will be faithful in praying for them as well as for their parents. When families return for furlough or home assignment, the MK is exposed to new people, unfamiliar places, a different culture and set of expectations, and thus also needs prayer in these areas. MKs need prayer for grace to relate to the many visitors in their homes as well as to those who host them.

REFLECTION

'I will be the God of all the clans of Israel.' Jeremiah 31:1

I do not believe that our heavenly Father will ever forget his children. I am a very poor father, but it is not my habit to forget my children. God is a very, very good father. It is not his habit to forget his children.

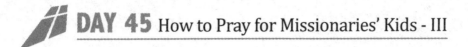

Personal Standards. The Missionaries' Kids (MKs) must develop godly principles and standards. They will need to be firmly grounded in God's word and develop their own values based upon it. The MKs need to adopt and maintain high biblical values in order to enable them to resist godless circumstances and pressure from their peers, the media and Satan. MKs must be taught to accept themselves, their bodies and their urges as part of God's plan. Healthy sexuality must be positively taught, first in the parents' acceptance of themselves, and then in parents initiating healthy discussions appropriate to the needs of the kids.

Pray that the MKs, if subjected to destructive temptations such as drugs, alcohol, sex, pornography and unedifying movies and videos, will resist them and set good examples for weaker peers; that when Satan tempts them they will resist him (James 4:7) and claim their position in Christ. Pray that they will view themselves as God's creation and walk in the light with Jesus in all relationships.

REFLECTION

'The Lord will watch over your coming and going.'
Psalm 121:8

We must trust in him; therefore we must seek to do his will. Preserved by him, we are as safe in the tempest as in the calm, on sea as on shore, beneath an eastern sky as in much-loved England. Without his protection we are safe nowhere, with it we are safe anywhere and everywhere.

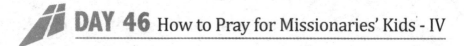

Cultural Adjustment. There is the continuing trauma of not quite belonging anywhere. When the Missionaries' Kid (MK) is serving with his parents, he is singled out as a foreigner, but when he returns to the so-called 'home country' he may not feel at home and may have difficulty fitting in. The MK needs to accept or at least tolerate different ways and customs and be willing to adapt. Language may also be a problem. Being able to cope is a great challenge to the MK.

Pray that the MKs will have an appreciation for the unique experiences they have had and that they might see how future ministry or vocation can be enriched by these experiences. Pray that the parents will help their children see their lives in a broad, global sense, encouraging them to consider ministry, whether at home or abroad, while being very careful not to put undue pressure on them. The Holy Spirit, through the scriptures, must lead the MK individually.

For Physical Safety and Health. Disasters such as typhoons, volcanoes, earthquakes, floods, drought, fires, as well as murders, kidnapping, robbery, unstable governments and hazardous travel threaten many missionary families. Many underdeveloped countries have very high pollution or lack adequate medical care or nutritious foods, causing some families to leave the field because of illness.

Pray that when MKs experience crisis situations their trust in God will not be shaken. Pray for safety. Pray for the measure of health that will best glorify our Lord. Pray for protection from indigenous and common diseases and that the MKs and their parents will remember that the only really safe place is in the will of God.

REFLECTION

'Pour out your hearts to him.'
Psalm 62:8

In the gladness of my heart I poured out my soul before God again and again confessing my grateful love to him who had done everything for me. I asked him to give me some work for him as an outlet for love and gratitude.

Dealing with Sin. Missionaries' Kids (MKs), like all kids, need to learn what sin is and how to deal with it victoriously. Due to circumstances on the field or at home, bitterness may develop. It must be recognised as sin, admitted, confessed, resisted and cleansed (1 John 1:9). When not dealt with, bitterness especially causes disastrous, long-lasting results (Hebrews 12:15).

Pray that the MKs, if guilty, will recognise and repent of their sins, i.e., bitterness, lying, stealing, cheating, unnecessary anxiety, sexual sins, worry or sinful anger. Pray that they will walk in the light with Jesus and not in the darkness with Satan from whom they have been freed. Pray that they will mature in Christ as they come into a deeper awareness of who they are in Christ and all that it means.

Satanic Influences. Satan, as the 'god of this world', uses the influences of the cultures in which we live and work to draw us away from the Lord.

Pray that parents will be prepared to provide strong spiritual defences for their families; that the MKs will learn early to exercise their authority as children of God to resist the attacks of the enemy; that they will choose the truth of God's word as their defence against the deceptions of Satan; that they will submit to God and resist the appeal of the world that opens the door to the activity of evil spirits; and that they will refuse the temptation to dabble in occult activities.

REFLECTION

'I press on toward the goal.'
Philippians 3:14

The accidents of ease or difficulty, of apparent safety or danger, of man's approval or disapproval, in no way affect our duty. Should circumstances arise involving us in what may seem special danger, I trust we shall have grace to manifest the reality and depth of our trust in Him and prove we are followers of the good shepherd who did not flee from death itself.

Finances. Many Missionaries' Kids (MKs) have been raised on limited financial resources (by home side standards), yet may have lived in very undeveloped countries where they may even have felt rich. This dichotomy has an effect on the MKs' view of wealth.

Pray they will accept their financial status without assuming attitudes of 'the world owes me a living' because their families have been supported by others; that MKs will not become bitter at the lack of 'things' while growing up; and that financial limitations will not cause them to make personal wealth their life goal.

Education and Development. MKs may not realise that their education on the field is often superior to that in their home countries, and that their cross-cultural experience is an education in itself.

Pray for homeschooled MKs: for protection of their study hours from undue interruption; arrival of their study materials in good time and condition; self-discipline for mothers in patiently holding children to their prescribed work; friendships outside the home; and the extra pressure on the mother.

Pray for MKs living at home and attending local national or international schools for: ability to keep up with classmates where possible or to accept themselves if they fall behind.

Pray regarding mission schools, that God will give special wisdom for mission leadership in regard to personnel who teach and care for the MKs, and wisdom in carefully supervising the school personnel.

Pray that MKs who are in a boarding school will adjust, get along with the house parents and other MKs, and look to the Lord when struck with homesickness. Pray that the caregivers will have godly wisdom to care for the spiritual and emotional as well as educational and physical needs of the MKs. Pray for MKs who have concerns, fears and anxieties about the future, in regard to their careers, further schooling, life partner etc.

Pray that the MKs will have assurance that the Lord will adequately meet their academic, social, school, emotional, and physical needs just as he is able to meet all their spiritual needs. Pray that the MKs will be protected from psychological, physical and sexual abuse in every situation.

Re-entry to the Home Country. Most Missionaries' Kids (MKs) re-enter their home country after completing high school. Proper re-entry is crucial to the MKs as they enter adulthood. They need to find a campus support group, friends who act as an extended family, and a supportive church, especially if they are not living with their relatives. It is important that they attend a re-entry seminar if at all possible to assist in the adjustment to a lifestyle that will often be different from the one with which they grew up.

Pray for good self-images rooted in their relationship with God that will not be threatened by cultural adjustments. Pray for keen observation skills; for a desire to know and understand others; for courage to ask appropriate questions and for a special friend to whom they can go for information and clarification. MKs often view the home-country kids as self-centred, affluent, shallow, fast-paced and unaware of the rest of the world. Pray that, rather than becoming cynical, the MKs will prayerfully choose their standards based on God's word and will not judge those around them.

Pray that they will demonstrate godly priorities and principles and influence others for Christ.

Pray that MKs will not be proud or withdraw in disappointment, but realise that the majority of their new friends have not had the opportunity to see the world as they have. Pray that God will give them boldness in sharing the things they have witnessed and the ways they have seen him work. Pray that they will take the challenge to inform and expose the church to world needs and not expect everyone to be excited about their lives and experiences as MKs.

ACCEPT YOUR RESPONSIBILITY.

Effective, strategic, specific, and regular prayer for MKs is absolutely essential. Missionaries do their part in fulfilling the Great Commission in obedience to Christ's command – it is essential that you as the prayer missionary accept responsibility for praying for the MKs effectively. Write to the MKs or to their families, find out about them, and let them know you care. Ask them for requests. Communicate regularly even if the MK doesn't write to you regularly. Use prayers in Scripture as a model for praying for MKs. Make the prayer personal by inserting the MKs' name or specific situation. (Ephesians 1:15-22, 3:16-21; Philippians 1:9-11; Colossians 1:9-14).

DAY 50 — Pastors Need Prayer, Too - I

God expects our pastors to take prayerful interest in our spiritual walk and the specific problems and needs of many. Consequently, the pastor carries a prayer burden for every person in his congregation. But who prays for his needs? He is human too and he needs our prayers. What a blessing when someone says to him in private, 'Pastor, you always have a place in my prayers and I'll be glad to pray for any special needs.'

A delegation of American pastors asked Charles Spurgeon the secret for his success. In response, Spurgeon led them to the lower level of his meeting house and quietly opened the door. The visitors saw over 400 people praying for God's blessing and power to rest upon their pastor who would stand in the pulpit to preach the word of God that night. 'There, gentlemen,' said Spurgeon, 'is the secret for God's blessing his work here'.

The Apostle Paul, a man of deep prayer, begged the church to pray for him. His ardent request was, 'I urge you, brothers ... to join me in my struggle by praying to God for me' (Romans 15:30, see also Ephesians 6:18–20; 2 Corinthians 1:8–12).

No matter how well you pay your pastor, praise him or work for him, it is only through earnest, strategic prayer that you can ever really help him be an effective minister in the hands of almighty God. Every pastor needs prayer for his personal needs, for spiritual wisdom and power, for his family and for overseeing God's flock (1 Peter 5:2).

Do not be overwhelmed by the number of suggested areas for prayer listed here; rather let the Holy Spirit lead you in making selections as you pray daily for your pastor and watch God work.

PERSONAL NEEDS.

True Humility. Pray that your pastor will keep a teachable spirit, that he will have the grace to receive criticism and profit by it, and that he will have a servant's heart. Pray that he will cultivate true humility in his walk, depending on God, not on his education, methods or personality. Pray that he would always pray and wait on God's leading and timing and then in both his successes and his failures, in all things, that he will be careful to give God all the glory. Pray against pride so that he will remain useable.

For special blessing and power to rest upon him as he preaches the Gospel. We join him in his struggles

Find real joy in his ministry, + peace Health mental + physical

Stability. Since we live in this carnal world with all its open and hidden pressures, pray that your pastor will keep his eyes on the Lord and serve with singleness of heart and will not become conceited over success or depressed by failure. Pray he will remember that Christians 'march to a different drum', that our value system is different from that of the world.

Relationships. Pray that your pastor will know how to deal with his own frustrations, with the lack of gifts in certain areas, with well-meaning but stubborn people in his congregation, and that he will walk in true brokenness, for it is no easier for a pastor to say, 'I am wrong', or 'I am sorry', than it is for anyone else. Pray that he will be patient with himself and others as he fulfils his varied responsibilities, that Calvary love will be shown in all interpersonal relationships and that he will sense the love and support of his congregation.

Joy. Pray that your pastor will find real joy in his ministry in spite of spiritual struggles and problems (John 16:24; 17:13). Joy is a significant hallmark of being filled with the Spirit – joy, great joy and peace, in the midst of and despite all circumstances (2 Corinthians 4:7–18; James 1:2–4; 1 Peter 1:6–9; Ephesians 5:18–21).

Health. Pray for your pastor's health and the lessons God will teach him in his time of sickness and recovery – resting in God's will and timing. Pray that he will maintain balance in exercise and recreation. Intercede, too, for safety as he travels.

Self-discipline. Since the pastor must prioritise and guard his time, be disciplined, and learn to say 'no', pray that the Holy Spirit will make him sensitive in these matters and that he will deal with role conflicts and stress in the Spirit and not in the flesh which results in burnout (see Matthew 11:30).

REFLECTION

'Our competence comes from God.'
2 Corinthians 3:5

The work is always increasing; and were it not for the consciousness of Christ as my life, hour by hour, I could not go on. But he is teaching me glorious lessons of his sufficiency, and each day I am carried onward with no feeling of strain, or fear of collapse.

FAMILY NEEDS.

Family Relationships. A pastor and his family live a kind of 'fish bowl' lifestyle. Therefore God's people need to respect the time they need as a family, and to pray that husband and wife will be devoted to one another and will be deeply related to each other. Pray that the pastor will maintain a scriptural family, seeking God's wisdom for the discipline of his children. Pray also for balance in time and attention given to his wife and children as he strives to provide good spiritual leadership for them.

Pressures. Pointed prayer is needed as your pastor and his family face daily temptations, stresses, peer pressures, and satanic attacks because they are special targets of the enemy. On the other hand, pray church leaders will recognise the personal, spiritual, physical, material and social needs of the pastor and his family so that they may not need to become overly preoccupied with the affairs of this life (2 Timothy 2:3–4; 1 Timothy 5:17–18).

REFLECTION

'He has given us his very great and precious promises.'
2 Peter 1:4

Like air and light, equally needful in every clime and in every circumstance, the promises and assurances of God's precious word meet us with help and comfort in all our various surroundings. It is our Father's will that his children shall be absolutely without worries.

SPIRITUAL NEEDS.

Spiritual Freshness. Pray that your pastor will 'walk in the light' with Jesus daily and depend on the Spirit's power in all phases of his life and ministry. Because his hardest job will be to keep spiritually fresh, pray that the pastor always remembers these facts concerning spiritual vitality: (1) the ministry is spiritual warfare, not just a job or a profession; (2) life's pressures will always result in spiritual decline unless he is careful to maintain a close walk with the Lord; (3) his need for spiritual enlightenment. Pray he continues to grow in Christ-like maturity, realising who he is in Christ, keeping short accounts with God.

Prayer. Pray that your pastor will understand that prayer is an absolute necessity and that he will prioritise his prayer life despite his very busy schedule. Over one hundred years ago, Lord Cecil said, 'The greatest menace to ministerial usefulness crouches at the door of the secret place.' Pray that your pastor will model an effective prayer life.

Integrity. Pray that he will resist moral temptation in line with who he is and whom he serves – the holy God, that his words and his actions will set a godly example and also that his thought life will glorify God and not pave the way for him and others to fall into immorality.

Spiritual Warfare. Above all, pray that your pastor will appropriate the full armour of God as outlined in Ephesians 6:10–18, being constantly aware of Satan's strategy at all times. Pastors are subject to the three-fold satanic temptation of the lust of the flesh, the lust of the eyes and the pride of life, just as everyone else (1 John 2:16). Pray that he will continually realise victory comes only through Christ, that he may have the word hidden in his heart and his armour on at all times and know how to use the sword of the Spirit in dealing with satanic opposition, oppression and possession.

Accountability. Pray that God will bless him with church leaders to whom he is accountable and that he will cultivate the friendship of at least one godly man (in or out of his congregation) to whom he will be especially open, transparent and spiritually accountable in all areas of his life and ministry. Pray that he will be keenly aware of the effects of his actions on the testimony of our Lord, on the church at large, on his own flock, as well as on his family and himself and, above all, aware of his accountability to God.

REFLECTION

'Worthy is the Lamb ... to receive ... glory and praise.'
Revelation 5:12

Do we sufficiently cultivate this unselfish desire to be all for Jesus, and to do all for his pleasure? Or are we conscious that we principally go to him for our own sakes, or at best for the sake of our fellow creatures? How much of prayer there is that begins and ends with the creature, forgetful of the privilege of giving joy to the creator.

CONGREGATIONAL NEEDS.

Pulpit Preparation. Since God's word and his Spirit do the lasting work in the church, pray that your pastor will give priority to study of the word and to prayer. Study in sermon preparation must not be a substitute for personal communion with God nor for a time of private worship. Lord Cecil also said, 'The greatest defect in the pastor's life is the lack of the devotional habit.' Pray for a prepared pastor as well as a prepared sermon, that his messages will not reflect human pressures but only the leading of the Holy Spirit, that the pastor will give a balanced presentation of scripture and not go off on tangents, and that he will present missions and evangelism as God's heart emphasises in the scriptures.

Christ-centred and Christ-exalting Preaching. Pray that the pastor's preaching will be less of him and more of Christ (Galatians 2:20), to edify the people and increase their love for Jesus and devotion to our Saviour. Pray that through it, God will show them how to develop a life of worship, and he will emphasise the need to go home and feed themselves.

Fruitful Relationships. Pray that in all his relationships the pastor will be discerning, open, flexible, understanding and forgiving, that he will be patient and make himself available to his people. Pray he will have a heart of compassion, and be a good listener, balancing tenderness with wisdom and firmness with love.

Individual Growth. Pray that with boldness, tenderness and love, your pastor will uncompromisingly confront sin. Pray his words will be loving, but firm and that the people will respond to the conviction of the Holy Spirit. Pray that he will preach for a response in changed lifestyles, that individuals will become progressively more Christ-like and not merely add to their store of biblical knowledge. Pray also that the pastor will deal with anything in his own life that is not in line with who he is and whom he serves (Matthew 18:15–35).

Mobilization. Also, pray that your pastor will encourage God's people in all the various stages of Christian growth and will help them discover their spiritual gifts by stepping out to fill a need. Pray that God will equip his people to train disciples and that the pastor will be absolutely committed to mobilising the gifts of the body.

Discernment. Pray for your pastor to have discernment in all areas including: (1) how to apply God's word to specific situations; (2) how to present biblical truth so that it will be understood and put into practice; (3) how to rightly assess and utilise the abilities and gifts of others. In view of the excessive demands on his time, pray that he will have discernment as to what God wants him to do and how God wants it done. Human discernment is always inadequate, but the mind of Christ is the sole judge for deciding what to say or do in all matters and actions: 'Do nothing out of selfish ambition or vain conceit' (Philippians 2:3–8). Pray for stability in the pastor's life, since it is so easy to be swayed by trends, fads and by winds of doctrine, and that he will keep balanced in all things. Pray that he will emphasise the need for all ages in the congregation to be united in love as God's family.

Counselling. Furthermore, pray that your pastor will not abandon his God-given right and responsibility to counsel his people in the wisdom of the Holy Spirit from the word of God and call them to repent from and deal with any sin in their lives. Pray that he will not feel that psychology and 'how-to' programmes, rather than the Bible, have the answers for today's troubled souls.

A FURTHER SUGGESTION

As you pray for your pastor you will discover that your hearts are knit together in a common purpose. You will understand that he, like Elijah, is 'a man, just like us' yet he is the man who has been appointed by the Holy Spirit as your pastor (Acts 20:28). Don't pray 'at him', but for him, and as you do, you will experience the marvellous way in which the Holy Spirit will bring to your mind special needs about which you should pray.

Finally, should you experience frustration in praying for your pastor, study and use the prayers of the Apostle Paul; they give much fuel for prayer. Please note: Ephesians 1:15–23, 3:14–21; Philippians 1:9–11; 2 Thessalonians 1:11–12 and 2 Corinthians 1:9–11.

'For this reason, since the day we heard about you, we have not stopped praying for you and asking God to fill you with the knowledge of his will through all spiritual wisdom and understanding. And we pray this in order that you may live a life worthy of the Lord and may please him in every way: bearing fruit in every good work, growing in the knowledge of God, being strengthened with all power according to his glorious might so that you may have great endurance and patience, and joyfully giving thanks to the Father, who has qualified you to share in the inheritance of the saints in the kingdom of light' (Colossians 1:9–12).

REFLECTION

'I have placed before you an open door.'
Revelation 3:8

Let but devoted labourers be found, who will prove faithful to God, and there is no reason to fear that God will not prove faithful to them. He will set before them an open door, and will esteem them of more value than the sparrows and the lilies that he clothes and feeds. He will be with them in danger, in difficulty, in perplexity.

Every teenager is under constant pressure from many sources. They are extremely vulnerable to all kinds of evil influences as this is the most difficult physical and emotional time of their lives.

At a time of life when many adults 'write them off' as irrational, uncontrollable, moody and unpredictable, God seeks to do a powerful work of drawing them to himself. Therefore there is a critical need for adult believers to be encouraged and equipped to pray for our youth. With so few godly role models or mentors, teenagers desperately need prayer if they are to grow and mature in Christ.

Teens must have God's power to live victoriously. Just saying 'No' is not enough. We need to pray Spirit-led, thoughtful, in-depth prayers for God to protect them before crises develop, as they fight major spiritual battles.

Salvation. In light of the troubled, antagonistic world in which teens live, pray that they will have assurance of their salvation, be fully aware of God's love for them, and not be ashamed to be called Christians.

Spirit-filled. The Lord commands us to be filled with the Holy Spirit (Ephesians 5:18). Nothing in the spiritual life is accomplished without his power and infilling. Pray that teens will be filled with the Spirit and therefore walk in the Spirit (Galatians 5:16, 25).

Grounded in the Word. It is essential that teens be grounded in the word of God if they are to mature spiritually. Pray that they will realise that in God's word there are truths to be believed, promises to be claimed, and commands to be obeyed. Pray that they will apply biblical principles in all areas of their lives, that they ask God to teach them to value prayer and that they will experience God's power. Pray that they will learn to renew their minds by memorising the word and use the scriptures to check out what is said and suggested by others.

Spiritual Maturity. Pray that as teens receive Christ as their Saviour, they will seek guidance and wisdom for their daily walk. Pray that the Holy Spirit will reveal to them all that they have and who they really are in Christ (Galatians 2:20; Romans 6–8). Pray that they will realise that Christ is in them and he is their life and that his calling is to a lifelong process of change, growth and maturity. Pray that they will increasingly be aware that God is all-powerful, has all knowledge and is everywhere.

Pray that teens will: (1) learn to love the Lord with all their heart, soul and mind, and serve and obey him; (2) know the Lord as the faithful provider and protector and trust him with every area of their lives; (3) grow in worshipping God through praise and thanksgiving.

REFLECTION

'Enoch walked with God.' Genesis 5:22

How important it is to us all, day by day, to be living for God, walking in holy friendship with Jesus, leaning on him as our strength and stay. The only preparation worth anything is that of the knowledge of God, of his word, and of communion with him who imparts his grace and strength to those who seek his face.

Need for Acceptance. Teens have a strong need to know they are loved for who they are, not for their looks, accomplishments etc. Pray that their parents, youth leaders, teachers and others will affirm them, that their role models/heroes will be godly and that teens will find their significance, acceptance and security in Christ. Many teens may feel that they have never received love, acceptance and affirmation in their homes, which can bring a sense of hopelessness. Suicide can often seem the only way out. Pray that God will protect them against consideration of suicide and that they will accept and honour their own families no matter what the problems and not compare them to other families.

Self-worth. Many teens have bought Satan's lie that their value comes from how well they succeed in the world and what others think of them i.e. physical appearance, performance, status, popularity etc. Pray they would see themselves as God sees them – holy, dearly loved, accepted, forgiven, new creations in Christ, children of God – not because of how they look but because of who they are in Christ Jesus. Pray they will realise their exalted position in Christ.

Teens are struggling with the whole issue of their identity. Who am I? What is my purpose in life? Am I worth anything? What makes me a valuable person? Pray that instead of being overwhelmed by confusion, they will trust Christ and appropriate all they have in him. Pray they will realise that God wants to change them through difficult circumstances and not necessarily change the circumstances, and that they will turn to Christ and not to various forms of sin when they suffer traumatic loss. Pray they will know to expect changes, and that in trials and temptations God has not promised an easy road, but He has promised His presence and control in all of life's circumstances.

Success can be the root cause of spiritual problems and lead to selfish pride. Failure can lead to depression. Pray that teens will not let success go to their heads, but give God the glory, that they will take a stand against Satan's effective tools of depression or pride. Pray that God will set them free from fear of failure, from comparison with others and from fear of being socially unacceptable or being thought different.

Peer Pressure. Specific prayer is needed as teens face daily temptations, stresses, peer pressure and satanic attacks. Pray that they will break from the world's self-centred culture and become Christ-centred, being daily transformed by the renewing of their minds (Romans 12:1–2). Pray that teens will have mental, emotional, doctrinal and moral stability. Pray they will realise their love for God is expressed through obedience to Him (John 14:15, 21–23).

REFLECTION

'Stop doubting and believe.' John 20:27

Lack of trust is at the root of almost all our sins and all our weaknesses; and how shall we escape from it, but by looking to him and observing his faithfulness? The man who holds God's faith will not be reckless or foolhardy, but he will be ready for every emergency.

Potential. Pray that teens will realise that Jesus calls them not because of who they are, but for what Christ has done and can do through them. Pray that they will decide to do their best in everything and reject a materialistic lifestyle. Pray that they will be selective in the music they listen to, will learn to pray for wisdom and will establish a biblical evaluation process. Pray that they will realise that the decision not to study, to experiment with sex or drugs, to engage in couch potato TV watching or pornography etc., can result in lifelong problems. Pray they will realise life is made up of choices between going God's way or their own way and that they are responsible for their choices. Pray they will see that God won't reveal his will in a specific situation unless they obey what they already know to be his will.

Leadership. Because today's teens are the next generation of Christian leaders, pray they will learn to be accountable, develop in honesty and integrity, and take care of their bodies, that they will equip themselves for Christian service.

REFLECTION

'Let me glean and gather after the reapers.' Ruth 2:7

Let us all leave the fatherland of the world, or at least become strangers and pilgrims in it. Where the need is greatest let us be found gladly obeying the Master's command. For it is in the harvest field, it is among the reapers, that we shall find him.

Forgiving. It costs to forgive, but the cost of not forgiving is much higher. Pray that teens will realise that when they have been hurt by someone, that person will continue to hurt them unless they forgive the offender, and that in Christ they can be free from the past. Pray that they will admit their own sin against others, ask them for forgiveness and make restitution if possible. Pray that since God forgives them, they must learn to forgive themselves.

Parents. Many teens come from dysfunctional or abusive homes. It is essential that teens know they are loved by their parents through actions as well as words. Teens don't care how much parents know until they know how much parents care. Pray for parents to speak the truth in love, not lecturing but asking the Lord to give opportunities to instruct when teens are most receptive. If teens do not feel accepted, a sense of insecurity can lead them into rebellious behaviour. Pray that parents will realise they can be godly parents only if they are godly persons and godly partners. Pray that they will exercise grace and patience while holding to God-directed limits to provide acceptance and security for their teens. Pray that parents will realise that hurting teens often react in anger and with unacceptable lifestyles, and to not take it personally. If teenagers do not have godly parents, pray for godly adult friends and role models to guide them with love and acceptance.

Rebellion. Frequently there is an attitude of 'I know it all' and 'nobody is going to tell me what to do', which can endanger their lives and their future. Pray against the spirit of rebellion and resistance to authority, which is so rampant at this age. Pray that teens will have a spirit of brokenness and humility, that pride will be broken and that they will deal with their sins through repentance (Psalm 51:7). Pray that they will have a willingness to see another's viewpoint.

REFLECTION

'"Not by might, nor by power, but by my Spirit," says the Lord Almighty.' Zechariah 4:6

Few of us, perhaps, are satisfied with the results of our work, and some may think that if we had more or more costly machinery we would be better. But I feel that it is divine power we want, not machinery! Wouldn't we do well to give ourselves to humiliation and prayer for nothing less than to be filled with the Spirit?

Temptation. The god of this world constantly seeks to lure teens away from simple and pure devotion to Christ (2 Corinthians 11:3). Pray that they will learn to take every thought captive to the obedience of Christ (2 Corinthians 10:3-5), and know that God's will is good, acceptable and perfect (Romans 12:2). They will only know this as they present their bodies (the word 'bodies' is key since most of what teens are tempted to do involves their bodies) as a living and holy sacrifice to God and have their lives transformed through the renewing of their minds (Romans 12:1-2). Pray they will learn that temptation is not sinning unless yielded to, that they will take responsibility for their wrong choices and not blame someone else, and that they will realise that through Christ is the only way they can effectively say 'No' to temptation. Pray they will learn to use scripture in resisting temptation and that God will especially guard them from sin that will affect them throughout their lives.

Purity and Personal Standards. As teens look for attention, affection and meaningful relationships, they can so easily fall into Satan's trap and yield to sinful desires and sexual immorality. Pray teens will realise that sex outside of marriage is sin and that there are physical, mental and spiritual prices to pay, often for a lifetime (AIDS,

pregnancy, bad memories). Pray that they will be taught healthy sexuality and that they will recognise the sinful fruit of much of TV, movies, videos and debasing music. Pray against Satan as he battles for their minds in all areas of purity. Pray they will be aware that their bodies are the temple of the Holy Spirit (1 Corinthians 6:19), that they will remember they reap what they sow (Galatians 6:7). Pray that they will fully realise they will have victory over the world, the flesh and the devil as they take the responsibility to say 'No' and let Christ live his life through them (Galatians 2:20; Romans 6).

REFLECTION

'You have been set apart to the Lord today.' Exodus 32:29

Let us trust him fully. Now if never before, now afresh if often before, let us take Jesus as our master and Lord, and with unreserved dedication give over to him ourselves, our possessions, our loved ones, our all. He is infinitely worthy and he will infinitely make up to us all we give to him.

Repentance and Sin. Teens need to learn what sin is and how to deal with it victoriously. Sin must be recognised, admitted, confessed and cleansed (1 John 1:9). When not dealt with, sin has disastrous, long-lasting results (Hebrews 12:15). Pray that teens will recognise, confess and repent of all known sin, that they will walk in the light with Jesus.

Witnessing to Others. With secular humanism in our education system, hostility to God on campus, and the antagonism of the media, we must pray that our youth will see through all of that and take Christ as their Saviour.

Pray for the Lord to raise up many teens to share and live the gospel in this ripe harvest field. Pray that churches and para-church groups will equip young people to be ambassadors for Christ (2 Corinthians 5:20), that the Holy Spirit will work in hearts and draw people to himself, and that teens humble themselves and admit their need for Christ. Pray that after they are saved, someone will effectively follow up with them, that they would make Christ the Lord of their lives.

Personal Relationships. Relationships are vital to the security, development, daily life and future of all teens. Pray they will develop wholesome relationships with their parents, use discernment in choosing their friends, especially those of the opposite sex, and be willing to break off all unhealthy relationships. Pray that they will resist the temptation to date non-Christians.

REFLECTION

'The one who feeds on me will live because of me.' John 6:57

Communion with Christ requires our coming to him. Meditating on his person and his work requires the diligent use of the means of grace, and especially the prayerful reading of his word. Many fail to abide because they habitually fast instead of feed.

Be Alert. Pray that teens will realise they cannot resist the devil (James 4:4) unless they submit to God. Both resistance and submission must be done to be fully effective. Pray that they would realise this requires a moment-by-moment decision.

Satan and the Occult. Satan, as the 'god of this world', uses the influence of the culture in which we live to draw us away from the Lord. Every young person hungers for spiritual reality and often desires to experience the world of the supernatural. Drugs and alcohol are artificial attempts to find that world, but they open the soul to satanic influences.

Pray against the lure of the occult, secret knowledge, special power and thrilling experiences. Pray against the dark influences of music, videos, magazines, books, movies, and TV that glorify Satan.

Pray that parents will provide strong spiritual defences for their families. Pray that teens will learn to exercise their authority as children of God, submit to him and resist the attacks of the enemy. Pray that they will choose the truth of God's word as their defence against the deceptions of Satan.

Pray that they will also remain aware of Satan's threefold strategy: the lust of the flesh (fulfilling our desires outside the will of God); the lust of the eyes (coveting that which God does not allow at a particular time or place); and the pride of life (self effort or independence from God). Pray that they will put on the whole armour of God (Ephesians 6:10–18).

HOW CAN I BE SURE I AM PRAYING EFFECTIVELY FOR TEENS?

• Accept responsibility and pray regularly and fervently for the specific needs of the teens the Lord lays on your heart.
• Ask the Holy Spirit for guidance as you pray.
• Pray with the authority you have in Christ, to bind the power of Satan (Mark 3:27).
• Pray the prayer of faith and claim victory (1 Corinthians 15:57–58).
• Use scripture as you pray (Ephesians 1:15–22, 3:16–21; Colossians 1:9–14).

REFLECTION

'If we walk in the light ... the blood of Jesus, his Son, purifies us from all sin.' 1 John 1:7

Are all your prayers answered? Does each morning bring you no fear? Is each day a psalm, each night a thanksgiving, sometimes sung in the minor keys – but still sung? Do your visitors feel impressed with the reality of the kingdom? Or, are there many things, some things, perhaps only one little thing, about which you claim to decide for yourself? Remember that only one such claim dethrones altogether your Lord and master, so far as lies in your power, no matter how trivial the matter may be.

ABOUT THE AUTHORS

J. Oswald Sanders

J Oswald Sanders was one of the twentieth century's most prominent Christian leaders and an internationally known Bible teacher, missionary leader and statesman. He was a prolific author whose public Christian ministry spanned seven decades.

Dr Sanders was a significant figure in the transformation of the China Inland Mission into the Overseas Missionary Fellowship, serving as General Director of the mission from 1954 to 1969. Under his leadership, the mission's ministry expanded from China into eight East Asian countries.

A systematic thinker, Sanders had a way of breaking down complex ideas into understandable segments. His books *Effective Faith* (OMF Books) and *Effective Prayer*, excerpted in this volume, are prime examples of the clarity and sharpness of his thought.

He authored over 40 books that have sold more than 2 million copies in 23 different languages. In 1980 Dr. Sanders was awarded the Order of the British Empire (OBE) by Her Majesty the Queen. In 1992 he accepted an honorary doctorate in theology from the Bible College of New Zealand. Dr. Sanders died in October 1992 at the age of 90.

James O. Fraser

James Otram Fraser began his missionary career in 1908. He was a diligent student of the Chinese language, a gifted Bible teacher, an accomplished musician and a dedicated man of prayer. He became interested in the mountain tribes in China and devoted himself to the Lisu, whose spoken language he mastered and reduced to writing for the first time, using a form of script he devised himself.

Fraser tirelessly gave himself to the Lisu, translating two of the Gospels into their language and in later years worked with others to translate the remaining New Testament. He laboured without ceasing on their behalf, making extensive journeys along the rugged mountain paths to visit the isolated villages. His love for them won their confidence and endeared him to them. In spite of physical hardship he was always willing to go wherever the voice of the Lord called.

Fraser was an avid personal writer and his journals have yielded a wealth of insights into his life of faith. Drawing extensively upon these journals, his biographer, Geraldine Taylor, crafted the classic biography *Behind the Ranges* (OMF Books), from the chapter 'The Prayer of Faith' which was excerpted. In recent times his daughter, Eileen Fraser Crossman, has compiled a biography entitled *Mountain Rain* (Shaw Publishers), portraying Fraser's timeless character and enduring faith.

Dr. Will Bruce

Wilbert H. Bruce is best known for his practical pamphlets on prayer. In all, the pamphlets are approaching the 2 million publication mark and are being translated into an increasing number of foreign languages. Bruce joined OMF International (formerly Overseas Missionary Fellowship) 40 years ago and spent 13 fruitful years in the Philippines, as well as many years on the home team as regional director and later as minister-at-large. Bruce and his wife, Jean, who are now with the Lord, left for Asia in December of 1959. While in the Philippines, they served in youth evangelism, radio work, literature distribution and training of nationals. He helped found Christ for Greater Manila, now known as Growth Ministries, and was involved in speaking at Bible conferences and evangelistic campaigns.

In May 1993, 42 years after being ordained to the ministry, Bruce received a Doctor of Divinity degree from Linda Vista Baptist College and Seminary in San Diego, California. His prayer pamphlets include *Why and How to Pray for Missionaries, Praying for One Another, Saturation Praying, O God Revive Us Again, Rescue Teens Through Prayer* and *Praying for Missionaries' Children.*

J. Hudson Taylor

Hudson Taylor was not only the founder of OMF International (formerly China Inland Mission), he was the father of the entire faith mission movement.

From his birth in 1832, Taylor was fascinated with China. By the age of 21 he had settled his course and was aboard the little clipper ship Dumfries bound for Shanghai. Out of deep respect and appreciation for the Chinese culture, he adopted Chinese dress in order to minister more effectively.

A physician by training, Taylor poured himself into treating the sick and preaching. Soon a fledgling church was established in Ningpo. However, in eleven of the eighteen provinces there was not a single Protestant missionary. In due time Taylor's vision of reaching inland China was realized, and the small band of 16 missionaries with whom he began the China Inland Mission in 1865 had swelled to a mighty army of almost 1400, becoming at one point the largest mission in the world.

Constantly busy with endless rounds of speaking engagements, personal visits, correspondence and the operation of the new mission, Taylor still began each morning with prayer. He had a profound influence on the life of the Church. By the time of his death in 1905, many mission agencies had adopted his methods and were seeing unparalleled fruit as a result.

A young Chinese evangelist fittingly expressed the scope of the gift Taylor left the Church in these words: 'Dear and venerable pastor, we too are your children. You opened for us the road to heaven. We do not want to bring you back, but to follow you.'

MORE IN THIS SERIES

ROMANS
Momentous News
By David Cook
ISBN: 978-1-906173-24-1

MARK
The Suffering Servant
By Jeremy McQuoid
ISBN: 978-1-906173-55-5

DANIEL
Far From Home
By Justin Mote
ISBN: 978-1-906173-68-5

1 THESSALONIANS
Living for Jesus
By Julia Marsden
ISBN: 978-1-906173-67-8

PHILIPPIANS
Press Towards the Goal
By Kay Mumford
ISBN: 978-1-909611-31-3

GALATIANS
The Life I Now Live
By Peter Mead
ISBN: 978-1-910587-09-6

ACTS
To the Ends of the Earth
By David Cook
ISBN: 978-1-909611-02-3

EZEKIEL
For His Glory
By Peter Lau
ISBN: 978-1-909611-83-2

JOHN
Never Thirst Again
By David Cook
ISBN: 978-1-909611-30-6

and more at... **10** Publishing
a division of 10 of those.com

To place an order call: **0844 879 3243** email: **sales@10ofthose.com**
or order online: **www.10ofthose.com**